wish

market to table

wish | market to table

Copyright © 2005 by CanWest Books,
representing CanWest Global Communications

Published by CanWest Books Inc.
A subsidiary of CanWest Global Communications
1450 Don Mills Road
Toronto, ON
Canada, M3B 2X7

Co-Published by St. Joseph Media

Library and Archives Canada Cataloguing in Publication

Wish the very best of food and entertaining : market
to table / editors: Andrea Stewart ... [et al.].

Contains index.
ISBN 0-9737410-4-X

1. Cookery. 2. Entertaining. I. Stewart, Andrea, 1967-
II. Title.

TX714.W564 2005   641.5   C2005-903878-0

Printed and bound in Canada by Solisco

First Edition

10 9 8 7 6 5 4 3 2 1

wish
market to table

Donna Dooher and Andrea Stewart with Suzanne Dimma and Jane Francisco

CANWEST BOOKS

contents

what a delicious year! Nothing defines our
cooking (and all else in our lives) better than the
influence of the four seasons. Through the pages of
wish magazine, we have delved into the simple allure
of market fresh ingredients, explored their preparations
and feasted on the results. Now we'd like to offer the best
of our first year and present it to you as an invitation to
spend more time sharing the pleasures of the table.
Off to the market...

jane, andrea, suzanne & donna

market fresh this season

artichokes

asparagus

dandelion greens

fava beans

fiddleheads

morel mushrooms

new potatoes

peas

radishes

ramps

rhubarb

sorrel

spring

thai beef noodle salad

grilled portobello mushroom salad

Thai Beef Noodle Salad

1	pound beef tenderloin, centre cut
1	tablespoon olive oil
1	tablespoon salt
1	teaspoon cracked black pepper
1	carrot, peeled and julienned
½	green papaya, peeled and julienned
2	tablespoons Thai basil leaves, chiffonade
¼	cup fresh mint leaves, chiffonade
¼	cup cilantro leaves
1	mango, peeled and cubed
1	English cucumber, peeled, seeded and cubed
1	cup bean sprouts
¼	cup peanuts (optional)
1	300 g-package glass noodles
1	cup Thai dressing (see page 141)

1. Preheat oven to 400 F, and place a baking sheet in oven to heat up.
2. Heat olive oil in a large sauté pan over medium-high heat. Season tenderloin with salt and pepper and sear beef, about 3 minutes each side. Remove from pan and place on preheated baking sheet. Roast for 15-20 minutes until rare. Remove from oven and allow to rest for 10 minutes before slicing into very thin pieces.
3. Place glass noodles in a bowl, and pour in enough boiling water to fully immerse. Let noodles soak for 5 minutes, stirring gently. Drain noodles. Toss with carrot, papaya, cucumber, mango, Thai basil, mint, cilantro, sprouts and most of the dressing. Heap noodle mixture onto a serving platter and arrange tenderloin slices over top. Drizzle entire dish with remaining dressing, and garnish with peanuts. **SERVES 6**

Nutrients per serving (includes dressing): *451 calories, 18 g protein, 12 g fat, 69 g carbohydrates, 5 g fibre.*

Grilled Portobello Mushroom Salad

2	tablespoons balsamic vinegar
2	tablespoons olive oil
1	teaspoon salt
½	teaspoon cracked black pepper
1	teaspoon minced garlic
12	small portobello mushroom caps
½	tablespoon fresh oregano leaves
¼	cup sundried tomatoes, julienned
6	cups baby arugula
½	cup sundried tomato vinaigrette (see page 141)
6	Parmesan tuiles (see page 140)

1. Whisk together the balsamic vinegar, olive oil, salt, pepper and garlic. Toss with mushroom caps and marinate for 10 minutes. Grill mushrooms, 2 minutes each side.
2. Toss baby arugula with ¼-½ cup of the sundried tomato vinaigrette. Lay 2 mushrooms in and around salad and garnish with julienned sundried tomatoes and oregano leaves. Top salad with a Parmesan tuile. **SERVES 6**

Nutrients per serving (includes dressing): *251 calories, 23 g fat, 7 g protein, 6 g carbohydrates, 2 g dietary fibre. Excellent source of vitamin E and riboflavin. Good source of folate, calcium and phosphorus.*

Walnut Parsley Pesto Pasta

2	cloves garlic
½	cup fresh Italian parsley leaves
¼	cup walnut pieces
¼	cup canola oil
3	Thai chilies (optional)
1	1-pound box rigatoni, cooked al dente

1. Place all ingredients except rigatoni into bowl of food processor and pulse until mixture comes together.
2. Toss with hot pasta. **SERVES 6**

Nutrients per serving: *681 calories, 23 g protein, 14 g fat, 119 g carbohydrates, 7 g fibre. Excellent source of magnesium and dietary fibre.*

walnut parsley
pesto pasta

colcannon potatoes

smoked tuna niçoise
in a potato cup

Colcannon Potatoes

8	Yukon Gold potatoes, peeled and quartered
¼	cup white vinegar
3	teaspoons salt
½	cup 2% milk, warm
¼	cup unsalted butter, cubed
1	pinch white pepper
1	pinch freshly grated nutmeg
3	cups finely sliced savoy cabbage, steamed until tender
2	green onions, thinly sliced
2	tablespoons chopped fresh Italian parsley

1. Place potatoes in a large pot, cover with cold water and add white vinegar and 1 teaspoon of salt. Bring to a boil, lower heat and simmer until completely tender, about 25 minutes. Potatoes are done when they can easily be pierced with a fork. Drain in a colander and let them steam-dry for 3 minutes.
2. Place potatoes back in pot, add warm milk and mash.
Chef's tip: For the creamiest results, use a food mill or potato ricer.
3. Mix in butter, remaining salt, white pepper and freshly grated nutmeg. Stir in savoy cabbage, green onions and parsley. **SERVES 8**

Nutrients per serving: 159 calories, 3 g protein, 9 g fat, 19 g carbohydrates, 2 g fibre. Excellent source of vitamin B₆.

Smoked Tuna Niçoise in a Potato Cup

12	mini new potatoes
1	tablespoon vegetable or grapeseed oil
6	slices smoked tuna, diced
¼	cup finely chopped red pepper
¼	cup finely chopped red onion
24	haricots verts (thin green beans), blanched
1	tablespoon spicy mayonnaise (see page 141)
1	small jar of black olive tapenade

1. Preheat oven to 400 F, and place a baking sheet in oven for 15 minutes.
2. Cut each potato in half. Using a melon baller, create a cup by hollowing out some of the potato. Cover potatoes in cold water until ready to use. Drain, pat dry and toss potatoes in oil.
3. Remove hot baking sheet from oven, place potatoes on baking sheet hollowed side down and return to oven. Cook for 15 minutes or until soft. Allow to cool.
4. Cut 1½ inches down from tip of bean, and set tips aside. Thinly slice remaining section of beans on the bias. Mix tuna with sliced beans, red pepper, red onion and mayonnaise in a bowl. Place tip of bean into potato cup. Fill with tuna mixture and top with black olive tapenade.
MAKES 24 PIECES

Nutrients per piece: 28 calories, 1 g protein, 1 g fat, 3 g carbohydrates, 0.3 g fibre.

vermicelli
vegetable rolls

Vermicelli Vegetable Rolls

1   package rice-paper wrappers
¼   cup cilantro leaves, picked
½   cup julienned red pepper
½   cup julienned yellow pepper
1   cup snow peas, stringed and julienned
1   cup bean sprouts
¼   cup pickled ginger
     sea salt and freshly ground black pepper
1   recipe seasoned vermicelli noodles (see right)
     orange-chili dipping sauce (see right)

1. In a large bowl filled with warm water, soak one rice-paper wrapper for about 20 seconds or until soft. Lay wrapper out on a tea towel to absorb excess water. Transfer wrapper to a flat surface.
2. About ⅓ from the bottom of the wrapper, create a 3-inch-long row with some cilantro leaves followed by some red pepper, yellow pepper, snow peas, bean sprouts, vermicelli noodles and a little ginger. Season with salt and pepper.
3. Carefully fold the bottom of the rice-paper wrapper over the vegetables. Turn in the sides and continue rolling up from the bottom.
4. To serve, slice the roll in half on a bias. Serve with Orange-Chili Dipping Sauce. **MAKES 12 ROLLS**

Seasoned Vermicelli Noodles

1   teaspoon sesame oil
1   teaspoon rice vinegar
1   cup cooked vermicelli noodles

In a medium-sized bowl, whisk together the sesame oil and rice vinegar. Toss cooked vermicelli noodles in sesame mixture. Set aside.

Orange-Chili Dipping Sauce

½   cup fresh orange juice
3   tablespoons granulated sugar
3   tablespoons soy sauce
2   teaspoons fresh lime juice
1   tablespoon sesame oil
1   tablespoon balsamic vinegar
1   teaspoon chili flakes
½   teaspoon salt

Whisk together all ingredients in a mixing bowl. Allow sauce to stand for 30 minutes for flavours to infuse. Serve at room temperature. This sauce will keep in a refrigerator for up to 2 weeks.

Nutrients per piece (with dipping sauce): 108 calories, 5 g protein, 1 g fat, 20 g carbohydrates, 1 g fibre. Excellent source vitamin C and folate. Good source of magnesium.

Chef's tip: Rice-paper wrappers can be found in Asian markets and at gourmet food stores. Soak one wrapper at a time and be gentle – they have a tendency to stick and tear.

classic *cooking 101* omelette

1. Crack 3 eggs into a bowl and whisk until yolks and whites are well combined.

2. Set an 8-inch omelette pan over high heat. When pan is hot, add 1 teaspoon butter. As butter begins to sizzle, pour in entire egg mixture. Using a high-heat spatula, stir slowly for 15-20 seconds as if you were making scrambled eggs.

3. Reduce heat to medium-low and place your fillings down the centre of pan (see our suggestions below). Use the handle of the pan as your guide to lay out ingredients.

4. As soon as the egg sets on the bottom (about 1 minute), fold $\frac{1}{3}$ of omelette to middle of pan, enclosing ingredients.

equipment

mixing bowl

whisk

high-heat spatula

8-inch omelette pan

ingredients

3 eggs
1 teaspoon butter

Try these fillings:
◆ Fresh, chopped tomato and your favourite grated cheese
◆ Sliced, cooked sausage and mushrooms
◆ Caramelized onion and goat cheese

5. To remove omelette from the pan and create the classic two-fold rolled effect, tilt pan, slide omelette out and use your spatula to create the final fold.

tomato ricotta &
chervil omelette

rainy day eggs

roast leg of lamb

Rainy Day Eggs

6	eggs
½	tablespoon unsalted butter
1	tablespoon all-purpose flour
1 ½	cups skim milk
½	teaspoon salt
1	tablespoon curry powder
3	green onions, finely chopped
	cracked black pepper

1. Place eggs in a pot and cover with cold water. Bring water to a boil and cook eggs for 7 minutes. Remove pot from heat, run eggs under cold water and set aside.
2. Melt butter, add flour and cook for 2 minutes. Add milk in a stream, whisking vigorously until mixture is thick and smooth. Add salt and cook for approximately 10-12 minutes until consistency resembles sour cream. Stir in curry powder.
3. Peel eggs and roughly chop. Combine the sauce with eggs and stir in green onions. Serve on crustless dry toast and sprinkle with cracked black pepper. **SERVES 4**

Nutrients per serving: 121 calories, 7 g fat, 9 g protein, 6 g carbohydrates.

Roast Leg of Lamb

1	leg of lamb, bone in, approximately 5 pounds
¼	cup olive oil
4	cloves garlic, thinly sliced
1	bunch of fresh rosemary, broken into 1-inch sprigs
3	teaspoons kosher salt
1 ½	teaspoons cracked black pepper
2	pounds new potatoes, halved
3	white onions cut into wedges

1. Preheat oven to 425 F.
2. Rub lamb with 3 tablespoons of olive oil. Make small incisions in meat and stud the leg by pushing pieces of garlic and sprigs of rosemary into each incision. Season with 2 teaspoons salt and 1 teaspoon black pepper.
3. In a large bowl, mix potatoes and onion with remaining olive oil, salt and pepper. Place lamb in a roasting pan, and spread potatoes and onions around the pan. Roast for approximately 1 ½ hours or until internal temperature reaches 140 F for medium rare. Remove from oven and let rest for 15 minutes before carving. **SERVES 6**

Nutrients per serving: 584 calories, 55 g protein, 22 g fat, 40 g carbohydrates, 5 g fibre. Excellent source of thiamin, vitamins B_6 and B_{12}.

Chef's tip: Roast lamb is traditionally served with mint sauce (see page 140), a perfect compliment to the rich flavour of the meat. Ovens vary widely in temperature (gas vs. electric, age of oven, etc.), so roasting times should be used as a guideline. Take the internal temperature for an exact measurement of doneness.

Ginger Carrots

12	baby carrots, blanched, tops left on
2	tablespoons finely chopped ginger
1	tablespoon brown sugar
1	tablespoon butter

Heat butter, sugar and ginger in a skillet. Add carrots and toss. Serve warm. **SERVES 2**

Nutrients per serving: 104 calories, 6 g fat, 1 g protein, 13 g carbohydrates, 1 g fibre. Excellent source of vitamins A and D.

ginger carrots

open-faced ricotta, pistachio & honey sandwich

crab fried noodles

Open-faced Ricotta, Pistachio & Honey Sandwich

6	½-inch slices of country bread
¾	cup ricotta cheese
½	cup pistachios
½	cup honey

1. Spread a generous layer of ricotta cheese on bread.
2. Sprinkle chopped pistachios on ricotta and drizzle with honey. **SERVES 6**

Nutrients per sandwich: 288 calories, 9 g fat, 8 g protein, 47 g carbohydrates, 3 g fibre, 196 mg sodium. Source of fibre. Good source of folate, thiamin, phosphorus and magnesium.

Crab Fried Noodles

2	tablespoons laksa paste (see page 139)
½	pound Chinese noodles, cooked
1	cup lump crab meat
½	cup bean sprouts
½	cup water chestnuts, chopped
½	cup snow peas, blanched
2	tablespoons Thai basil

1. Warm laksa paste over medium heat in a large sauté pan.
2. Add remaining ingredients. Mix and heat thoroughly.
SERVES 4

Nutrients per serving: 143 calories, 9.3 g protein, 2 g fat, 21 g carbohydrates, 2 g fibre. Good source of folic acid and iron.

spatchcock cornish hen

Spatchcock Cornish Hen

- 2   Cornish hens
- 4   lemons, sliced in half
     smoky citrus rub (see page 141)

1. To spatchcock the hens, lay them on a cutting board breast-side down. With poultry shears, cut along one side of the backbone up to the neck. Then cut along the other side of the backbone and remove neck and spine. Press down to flatten. (See A-Z Culinary Guide, page 142, for step-by-step pictures.)

2. Massage the entire hen with dry rub. Place on grill over medium high heat, skin-side down and cook for approximately 10 minutes. Continue to grill for 20 more minutes, turning as needed to develop colour and crispiness.

3. For the last few minutes of grilling, lay the halved lemons pulp-side down directly onto the grill to char. Serve with hens. **SERVES 4**

Nutrients per serving: 310 calories, 21 g fat, 26 g protein, 5 g carbohydrates, 2 g fibre. Excellent source of niacin. Good source of vitamins B_6, B_{12} and C, iron, zinc and phosphorus.

Snip

Snip, snip

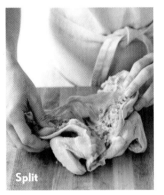

Split

Flatten

Rub

you say butterfly, we say spatchcock!

Spatchcock is another term for butterflying poultry. By removing the backbone of the bird and flattening it, the bird can be grilled without using a spit.

breakfast in bed

Surprise your sweetheart with a true indulgence.

decadent
love

mimosas
eggs
sausages
crepes
hot mocha

healthy love

oatmeal
soft-boiled eggs
pomegranate juice
fresh fruit

☐ **Less time in the kitchen, more time in bed.** Waltz into the bedroom with the ease of Nigella Lawson and the style of Jacqueline Kennedy. Plan ahead and keep things simple. There are many delicious products available at your favourite shops and supermarkets to take the pressure off the stove. Do as much as you can the night before.

☐ **Garden of love.** Top off your breakfast tray with a collectible vintage teacup filled with small flowers or sprouts.

healthy love

1. Warm your hearts and toes by sharing a big bowl of hot oatmeal topped with dried fruit, nuts or muesli, and a sweet sprinkle of brown sugar. **2.** Serve with soft-boiled eggs, fresh-fruit salad, pomegranate-grapefruit juice and brewed coffee.

Get in the Mood: Fresh & Fun
A combination of chartreuse, yellow and pale-blue stripes makes for a fresh summertime look that sets the scene for a healthy breakfast.

(previous page)

decadent love

1. Fuel the passion with a full breakfast – grapefruit mimosas, white hot mocha, sunny-side-up eggs, plump cherry tomatoes and chorizo sausage for a little spice. **2.** Keep the heat on high with crepes (see page 138) smothered in a long, slow pour of maple syrup.

Get in the Mood: Lush & Romantic
Layers of toile, patchwork and lush floral imagery combine with flea-market finds to create the mood for a decadent breakfast. The menu is so plentiful, you might need two trays.

breakfast at tiffany's

- ☐ **Girl's best friend.** Treats inside a little blue box are always a hit. This one gets personalized with a card to match the decor.

- ☐ **Your heart on a string.** Simple hearts cut from red bristol board or old Valentine cards and strung from fine wires can be tacked to the ceiling to add romance and fun. Use fun tack if you're worried about damaging paint. **Tip:** Tape a loonie between two hearts to give your creation some weight.

continental love

1. Pop over to your favourite bakery for buttery croissants and the specialty grocer for a wedge of artisan cheese. **2.** The sensual shape of the miniature Forelle pears conjures up romantic notions, and strawberries are perfect little bites to share. **3.** French-pressed coffee and fresh-squeezed orange juice add a cosmopolitan flare.

Get in the Mood: Modern Cosmopolitan
Basic black-and-white bedding is a classic. A graphic pillow and maple wood accents give the room a contemporary edge – the perfect backdrop for an easy-to-prepare continental breakfast.

continental love

fresh-squeezed oj
croissants
berries & forelle pears
french-pressed coffee

market fresh this season

apricots

blackberries

blueberries

cherries

green & yellow beans

peaches

raspberries

saskatoon berries

strawberries

swiss chard

tomatoes

zucchini

summer

fancy leftover
lambwich

tuscan white bean crostini

Fancy Leftover Lambwich

Leftovers can sometimes be better than the dinner itself. Use **leftover lamb** or other roasted meat, **naan bread** (pita and tortilla wraps also work well), **grilled red onions** and your **favourite greens**. If you have any leftover **mint sauce** (see page 140) or **chermoula marinade** (see page 138), just stir it into some **mayonnaise** and spread it on.

Tuscan White Bean Crostini

2   tablespoons olive oil
1   large shallot, finely chopped
2   cloves garlic, minced
2   cups canned white beans, drained
6   fresh sage leaves
2   tablespoons extra-virgin olive oil
1   teaspoon salt
1   tablespoon fresh lemon juice
1   whole wheat baguette, cut into ½-inch slices

1. Heat olive oil in a sauté pan over medium heat. Add shallots and garlic and cook until soft. Add white beans and cook for 1 minute.
2. Transfer mixture to a food processor. Add sage leaves, extra-virgin olive oil, salt and lemon juice. Purée until smooth. Spread on toasted baguette. **MAKES 2 CUPS**

Nutrients per piece: *68 calories, 2 g fat, 2 g protein, 9 g carbohydrates, 1.5 g fibre.*

Chef's tip: To dress up crostini, fry whole fresh sage leaves in a small amount of vegetable oil for 30 seconds. Drain on paper towel.

Tomato Tarte Tatin

½   recipe short-crust pastry (see page 110)
3   tablespoons granulated sugar
2   tablespoons balsamic vinegar
2   tablespoons unsalted butter
1   tablespoon chopped fresh thyme
8   Campari tomatoes (you can substitute plum tomatoes but they are slightly larger and you will need a larger tart shell)

1. Preheat oven to 425 F.
2. Heat sugar and vinegar in a small saucepan, stirring until sugar dissolves. Simmer until slightly syrupy, about 3 minutes. Remove from heat and stir in butter and thyme, mixing until butter has melted. Distribute sauce evenly among eight 2½" x ³⁄₄" disposable aluminum tart shells.
3. Roll out pastry to ⅛-inch thickness and cut into 2½-inch circles.
4. Take one whole tomato in the palm of your hand. Cover the top half of the tomato with a pastry disc and gently shape the disc to the curve of the tomato. Half of the tomato should be covered. Place pastry-wrapped tomato into the tart shell with the pastry facing up.
5. Place tart shells on a sheet pan and bake for 10 minutes. Lower oven temperature to 375 F and rotate sheet pan. Continue cooking for 10 more minutes.
6. Allow tarts to rest for 1-2 minutes. To serve, flip each tart shell upside down on a plate. Now the pastry is on the bottom and the delicious cooking juices will spill over the tomato. **MAKES 8 TARTS**

Nutrients per tart: *115 calories, 3 g fat, 2 g protein, 20 g carbohydrates, 2 g fibre. Good source of vitamin C, folate and thiamin.*

tomato tarte tatin

green papaya salad

golden gazpacho

Green Papaya Salad

2	limes, juiced
2	tablespoons granulated sugar
2	tablespoons fish sauce
1	clove garlic, minced
1	small Thai chili, finely chopped
1	cup long beans, cut into $1/2$-inch pieces
4	cups green papaya, julienned
8	cherry tomatoes, halved
$1/4$	cup unsalted peanuts, roughly chopped

1. Combine lime juice, sugar and fish sauce, and stir until sugar is dissolved.

2. In a separate bowl, mix garlic, Thai chili and long beans together. Add green papaya and cherry tomatoes. Mix thoroughly. (If you like really spicy food, increase the amount of Thai chili.)

3. Toss with the lime and sugar mixture and pile onto a large platter. Garnish with peanuts. **SERVES 8**

Nutrients per serving: 104 calories, 3 g protein, 3 g fat, 18 g carbohydrates, 3 g fibre. Excellent source of vitamin C.

Golden Gazpacho

2	cloves garlic
25	yellow tomatoes, blanched, peeled and seeded
1	Vidalia onion, finely chopped
2	yellow peppers, finely chopped
$1/2$	cup fresh lime juice
3	tablespoons sherry vinegar
$1/2$	cup finely chopped cilantro
2	tablespoons finely chopped jalapeno peppers
2	teaspoons kosher salt

1. Preheat oven to 350 F.

2. Wrap garlic in aluminum foil and roast until soft, about 20 minutes. Let cool.

3. Finely chop tomatoes and place in a large mixing bowl with all their juices.

4. Using the back side of a chef's knife, crush the roasted garlic into a paste and add to tomatoes. Mix in remaining ingredients and season with salt. Refrigerate until ready to serve. **SERVES 8**

Serving tip: Drizzle with extra-virgin olive oil or tangerine oil just before serving.

Nutrients per serving: 143 calories, 4 g fat, 7 g protein, 27 g carbohydrates, 6 g fibre. Very high source of fibre. Excellent source of vitamins B_6 and C, folate, niacin, thiamin, iron and magnesium. Good source of riboflavin, zinc and phosphorus.

pickled ginger tuna pita

homemade lemonade

Pickled Ginger Tuna Pita

¼ cup pickled ginger, finely chopped
¼ cup rice vinegar
¼ cup mirin
⅓ cup grapeseed oil or canola oil
1 can tuna, drained
1 tablespoon black sesame seeds
1 pita, cut in half
1 handful alfalfa sprouts

1. Whisk together pickled ginger, rice vinegar and mirin. Slowly add oil until combined.
2. Mix ¼ cup of vinaigrette (save any extra in the fridge) with tuna and black sesame seeds. Stuff each half of the pita with tuna mixture. Top with sprouts. **MAKES 1 PITA**

Chef's tip: Keep tuna interesting by changing the vinaigrette. Try sundried tomato, citrus or wasabi vinaigrettes.

Nutrients per ½ pita: 299 calories, 12 g fat, 26 g protein, 19 g carbohydrates, 1 g fibre. Excellent source of vitamin B_{12} and niacin. Good source of vitamin B_6, folate, thiamin, iron, phosphorus and magnesium.

Homemade Lemonade

1 cup granulated sugar
5 cups cold water
1¼ cups fresh lemon juice (about 5 lemons)

1. In a stainless-steel saucepan, combine sugar and 1 cup of water. Bring to a boil, stirring until sugar has dissolved. Reduce heat and simmer for 5 minutes. Remove saucepan from heat and let sugar syrup cool completely.
2. Stir in lemon juice and remaining 4 cups of water to cooled sugar syrup. Refrigerate lemonade until cold. Garnish with sprigs of mint or lemon balm. **SERVES 6**

Cooler Variations

For Adults: Use sparkling water instead of tap, and add 6 ounces of vodka. Try citron- or raspberry-flavoured vodkas to enhance the taste even more.
For Kids: Drop in a maraschino cherry and a splash of cranberry juice for pink lemonade.
"Instant" Iced Tea: Add some of your homemade lemonade to cold brewed tea. No undissolved sugar in the bottom of your glass and no squirting lemon in your eye!

cooking 101
sushi: maki

equipment

bamboo mat

sharp knife

ingredients

1   nori sheet

1   cup cooked sushi rice

½   cucumber

¼   avocado

2   ounces sushi-grade tuna, mackerel or salmon

1. Prepare sushi rice (see page 141). Thinly slice your fillings. Cut fish in lengths to fit nori, about ¼-inch thick.
2. Lay out bamboo mat and place one nori sheet on top, lining up the edge closest to you.
3. Place approximately 1 cup sushi rice at edge of nori sheet. Dip your fingertips in water and shake off excess. Using just the tips of your fingers, begin pushing the rice out to evenly cover nori, leaving at least ½ inch at the edge farthest from you. If necessary, moisten fingertips again.

4. Lay strips of fillings and fish across the rice approximately ⅓ of the way up from the edge closest to you. Be sparing with fillings or the roll will become thick and hard to manage. Lift up the edge of the bamboo mat closest to you and pull over the fillings. Now begin to roll nori using the bamboo mat.
5. Dip the tip of a very sharp knife in water and hold blade upright to allow excess water to dampen length of the blade. This will allow the blade to make a clean cut through the roll and minimize sticking. Wipe the blade after each cut and dip again. Slice the roll into 6 even pieces and serve with the appropriate garnishes (see right).
6. Practice makes perfect.

Sushi Service

Soy Sauce or Shoyu

Made by fermenting soybeans, wheat, salt and water. It is widely used to flavour dishes and as a dipping sauce for sushi.

Sushi Rice

A short-grained, starchy rice used specifically for sushi.

Pickled Ginger

This condiment cleanses the palate between bites and between courses.

Wasabi

Very hot Japanese horseradish. Purchase either as a powder or pre-made paste. Add a small amount to soy dipping sauce to spice things up.

Nori

Sheets of toasted seaweed. They are rich in calcium, iron, proteins, vitamins and minerals, and are subtle in flavour.

tuna maki

chipotle garlic-rubbed chicken

yukon gold frites

Chipotle Garlic Rub

Super hot and spicy – great for steak, ribs or chicken.

- 3 tablespoons canned chipotle peppers, finely chopped
- 2 tablespoons minced garlic
- 1 tablespoon dried parsley
- 1 teaspoon salt
- 2 teaspoons ground cumin
- 1 teaspoon ground oregano
- 2 tablespoons olive oil

Combine all ingredients in a small bowl and mix well. (See Pantry Extras, page 136, for more rubs and marinades.)

Nutrients per serving: 74 calories, 7 g fat, 1 g protein, 3 g carbohydrates, 1 g fibre.

Yukon Gold Frites

- 6 Yukon Gold potatoes, unpeeled and cut into thick matchsticks
- 6-8 cups sunflower oil

1. Soak potatoes in cold water for a minimum of 1 hour, or even the day before, and refrigerate.
2. Using a deep fryer or wok, heat sunflower oil to 250 F.
3. Drain and pat potatoes dry with a paper towel. Par-cook potatoes in the hot oil for approximately 5 minutes or until potatoes are slightly cooked but no colour has developed. Drain on paper towels.
4. Raise heat of oil to 375 F and drop in par-cooked fries. Cook until golden, 3-5 minutes. Season generously with salt.

Nutrients per 3-ounce serving: 319 calories, 5 g protein, 17 g fat, 38 g carbohydrates, 4 g fibre. Excellent source of vitamins B_6 and C.

The Healthiest Hamburger

- 1 tablespoon canola oil
- 3 cloves garlic, minced
- 1 cup finely chopped shallots
- ½ cup flaxseed
- 1 tablespoon mustard seeds
- 1 omega-3 egg
- ½ cup bread crumbs or panko
- 1 teaspoon cracked black pepper
- 2 teaspoons kosher salt
- 2 pounds ground bison meat

1. Heat oil in a sauté pan over medium heat.
2. Cook shallots and garlic until soft but not brown. Set aside to cool.
3. Using a mortar and pestle, pound flaxseed and mustard seeds until they begin to break down. Alternatively, gently pulse in a food processor.
4. In a large bowl, combine all ingredients with bison meat, and shape into 4 patties.
5. Grill or fry patties to medium-rare.

MAKES FOUR 8-OUNCE BURGERS

Nutrients per patty: 671 calories, 51 g protein, 40 g fat, 25 g carbohydrates, 7 g fibre, 4 g omega-3. Excellent source of iron, zinc and dietary fibre.

Chef's tip: Serve this omega-3-packed patty on a whole-grain bun with grainy dijon mustard and purslane for an extra kick of fibre and fatty acids.

the healthiest hamburger

panzanella salad

grilled summer squash

Panzanella Salad

1   loaf Italian bread, sliced into $\frac{1}{2}$-inch cubes (about 4 cups)
$\frac{1}{4}$ cup red-wine vinegar
$\frac{3}{4}$ cup extra-virgin olive oil
1   teaspoon sea salt
1   teaspoon cracked black pepper
1   small red onion, thinly sliced
2   pints cherry tomatoes (red and yellow), cut in half
1   bunch fresh basil leaves, torn into small pieces
$\frac{1}{4}$ cup caperberries or capers, drained

1. Preheat oven to 325 F.
2. Place bread cubes on a baking sheet and toast for 5 minutes.
3. In a large salad bowl, whisk together vinegar, olive oil, salt and pepper. Add toasted bread and toss.
4. Mix red onion and tomatoes into bread mixture and let stand for 30 minutes at room temperature.
5. Just before serving, toss in basil leaves and caperberries.
SERVES 8

Nutrients per serving: 256 calories, 21 g fat, 3 g protein, 15 g carbohydrates, 2 g fibre. Excellent source of vitamin E. Good source of folate.

Grilled Summer Squash

3   cups pattypan squash
1   cup baby zucchini
1   small red onion, diced
2   tablespoons olive oil
2   tablespoons chopped fresh Italian parsley
1   tablespoon lemon zest
    salt and pepper

1. Toss squash, zucchini, onion, olive oil, salt and pepper together in a bowl.
2. Transfer to vegetable grilling basket and grill over medium-high heat for approximately 10 minutes.
3. Remove from basket and mix in parsley and lemon zest.
SERVES 6

Nutrients per serving: 67 calories, 5 g fat, 1 g protein, 6 g carbohydrates, 2 g fibre.

brandied chicken liver
frisée salad

fresh herbs

Brandied Chicken Liver Frisée Salad

1	pound chicken livers, trimmed and cut in half
2	tablespoons clarified butter
¼	cup all-purpose flour, seasoned with 1 teaspoon salt
1	tablespoon brandy or cognac
6	cups frisée
½	cup Dijon Vinaigrette (see page 139)
	Glazed Pearl Onions (see page 139)

1. Pat livers dry with a paper towel. Dredge in flour and set aside on a plate.

2. In a large sauté pan over high heat, add one tablespoon of clarified butter. When pan is hot, add half of the livers and cook for 3 minutes or until golden. Flip and finish cooking for another 2 minutes. Repeat with remaining butter and livers. Deglaze with brandy or cognac and return livers to pan to keep warm.

3. Toss frisée with vinaigrette and set in middle of platter. Top with warm livers and glazed pearl onions. **SERVES 4**

Nutrients per serving: 274 calories, 15 g protein, 17 g fat, 13 g carbohydrates. Excellent source of vitamins A and B_{12}, zinc and iron.

beach barbecue

Nothing beats the heat like a long, cool drink in the great outdoors
– and alfresco dining is the perfect way to end a summer's day.
A view of the setting sun only adds to the perfection.

the menu
lemonade
coleslaw
orzo salad
bbq ribs
watermelon
grilled peaches

sunset dinner checklist

☐ **Menu planning is important.** Choose dishes that can be prepared several hours in advance or even the day before. This will allow you to spend more time with your guests enjoying the view.

☐ **Have an extra tank of propane** or bag of charcoal on hand just in case.

☐ **Cook extra.** That way, you'll have leftovers and won't have to worry about lunch the following day.

☐ **Pre-cooked and marinated ribs** are easy to find at the local grocer.

☐ **Packaged coleslaw will save you** chopping in the kitchen and cleaning a food processor.

☐ **Use colour-coordinated tea towels** as placemats.

☐ **Candlelight adds sparkle to a table** while the sun sets. Use citronella candles to help keep the bugs away.

☐ **Keep a cooler of ice and drinks close by** so you don't have to keep running into the house.

orzo salad

Orzo Salad

This salad tastes even better when you make it a day ahead of time. Just add the fresh basil before serving.

1½	cups orzo pasta, cooked al dente
½	cup extra-virgin olive oil
½	cup red-wine vinegar
1	teaspoon salt
1	roasted red pepper, diced
1	roasted yellow pepper, diced
½	cup pine nuts, toasted
1½	cups fresh basil leaves, torn into large pieces
½	cup finely diced red onion
1	cup crumbled feta cheese

1. Toss the cooked pasta with the olive oil, red-wine vinegar and salt. Stir in the peppers, pine nuts, onion and basil.
2. Sprinkle with the feta cheese. Serve at room temperature. **SERVES 8**

Nutrients per serving: 484 calories, 28 g fat, 19 g protein, 46 g carbohydrates, 13 g fibre. Excellent source of vitamins C and E, folic acid, niacin, thiamin, riboflavin, calcium, phosphorus, magnesium and zinc.

iced watermelon &
homemade lemonade

grilled summer peaches

barbecued back ribs

Iced Watermelon

Keep watermelon whole and in the fridge until you are ready to serve it. Cut into easy-to-hold wedges and layer with crushed ice for a refreshing palate cleanser.

Grilled Summer Peaches

8	large peaches, firm but ripe
1/3	cup unsalted butter, melted
1/3	cup granulated sugar

1. Halve and pit peaches.
2. Combine melted butter with sugar, stirring to dissolve. Brush each peach half with butter/sugar mixture and grill over medium heat until browned in spots and warmed through. **SERVES 8**

Nutrients per serving: 138 calories, 8 g fat, 1 g protein, 18 g carbohydrates, 2 g fibre.

rib school

Most butchers have great pre-marinated ribs to save you time. You can always add your own barbecue sauce while they are on the grill.

Cooking: Metal grilling racks are excellent gadgets to have for cooking ribs on the barbecue. They allow you to cook your ribs without having to continually flip them. **Chef's tip:** Ribs will stay hot for up to one hour if you place them in a loose-fitting paper bag and close it tightly.

Portioning: Serve 1/3 of a side per person.

Serving: Plate each portion for guests and have a platter with extras to pass around for those with an appetite. Don't forget an empty bowl for the bones and finger bowls for fast cleanup.

market fresh this season

- apples
- brussels sprouts
- celery root
- corn
- grapes
- leeks
- parsnips
- pears
- potatoes
- red peppers
- squash
- tomatoes
- turnips

fall

baked squash &
apple salad

smoked trout, fennel &
celery root salad

Baked Squash & Apple Salad

2	small pepper or acorn squash
2	teaspoons kosher salt
2	tablespoons clarified butter
2	apples, Granny Smith or Cortland
6	cups mixed salad greens
¼	cup pine nuts, toasted
⅔	cup warm cider dressing (see page 138)

1. Preheat oven to 400 F.
2. Cut squash in half lengthwise and remove seeds.
Cut each half into 1-inch thick slices, lengthwise.
3. Line a baking sheet with parchment paper and spread squash out. Season with salt and bake for 15 minutes. Turn slices over and bake for another 15 minutes or until golden and tender.
4. Peel apples and cut in half lengthwise. Remove core and cut each half into four wedges. Sauté apples in clarified butter until golden brown. Set aside.
5. Distribute greens on 6 plates and arrange squash and apple slices over top.
6. Using the cider dressing, deglaze sauté pan that apples were cooked in, and reduce to a syrupy consistency.
7. Drizzle warm dressing over greens, and sprinkle with pine nuts. **SERVES 6**

Nutrients per serving: 257 calories, 4.5 g protein, 9 g fat, 40 g carbohydrates, 6 g dietary fibre. Good source of vitamins A, B_6 and C.

Smoked Trout, Fennel & Celery Root Salad

1	small red onion, thinly sliced
3	cups julienned celery root
1	medium fennel bulb, thinly sliced
1	Granny Smith apple, peeled, cored and cut into matchsticks
4	smoked trout, skin removed, broken into 1-inch pieces
2	bunches watercress
1	cup remoulade (see page 140)
¼	cup chive oil (see page 138)

1. Soak onion slices in cold water. Toss celery root, fennel and apple together in a large bowl. Drain onion and add to celery root mixture. **Chef's tip:** The cold water soaking helps remove the onion's bitterness.
2. Mix in remoulade, tossing to coat evenly and season with salt and pepper.
3. Arrange a bed of watercress on each plate, top with celery root mixture and garnish with smoked trout and chive oil. **SERVES 8**

Nutrients per serving: 576 calories, 5 g protein, 57 g fat, 15 g carbohydrates, 3 g fibre. Good source of vitamins B_6, B_{12} and C.

Roma Tomato Sauce

½	cup olive oil
3	cloves garlic, minced
1	large white onion, chopped
1	teaspoon chili flakes
8	cups blanched and peeled Roma tomatoes or two 28-ounce cans whole plum tomatoes, juice included
¼	cup tomato paste
1	tablespoon granulated sugar
¼	cup extra-virgin olive oil
1	tablespoon chopped fresh marjoram
1	tablespoon chopped fresh basil
1	tablespoon salt

1. Warm olive oil in a large stainless-steel pot. Add garlic, white onions and chili flakes, and cook over medium heat for about 5 minutes until softened but not browned. Add tomatoes, tomato paste and sugar. Cook, stirring occasionally, over medium-low heat until sauce has thickened, about 20 minutes.
2. Remove from heat and allow tomato sauce to cool slightly.
3. Purée sauce in a food processor or pass through a food mill. Add extra-virgin olive oil, herbs and salt.
4. Reheat to use in your favourite recipe or refrigerate, freeze or can. **MAKES 6 CUPS**

Nutrients per ½ cup: 164 calories, 14 g fat, 2 g protein, 10 g carbohydrates, 2 g fibre. Good source of vitamin C.

roma tomato sauce

mushroom oregano rice

stacked BLT & avocado salad

Mushroom Oregano Rice

½ pound unsalted butter
3 cups finely chopped onion
2 cups long-grain rice
2 cups white mushrooms, quartered
1 green pepper, diced
3 cans beef consommé
2 cans water, using consommé cans to measure
2 teaspoons roughly chopped fresh oregano

1. Preheat oven to 350 F.
2. Melt butter in a large pot, add onions and cook until golden. Add rice and continue to cook until rice is also golden. Stir in mushrooms and green peppers, cooking for 5 more minutes.
3. Place into a 9" x 13" baking dish and add consommé, water and oregano. Cover with aluminum foil and bake for 1 hour until rice is cooked through. **SERVES 6**

Nutrients per serving: 550 calories, 31 g fat, 7 g protein, 61 g carbohydrates, 3 g fibre.

Stacked BLT & Avocado Salad

4 large tomatoes, mix of red and yellow
1 avocado, halved, pit and skin removed
8 slices pancetta, cooked crispy
1 cup arugula
4 teaspoons extra-virgin olive oil
   salt and pepper

1. Slice tomatoes ¼-inch thick and lay out in a single layer. Season with salt and pepper.
2. Cut avocado halves into eight slices lengthwise.
3. Layer tomatoes alternating with pancetta, arugula and avocado slices.
4. Drizzle each stack with 1 teaspoon extra-virgin olive oil.
SERVES 4

Nutrients per serving: 394 calories, 37 g fat, 10 g protein, 10 g carbohydrates, 4 g fibre. High source of fibre. Excellent source of vitamin E and folate. Good source of vitamin C and magnesium.

Chef's tip: To capture the essence of an authentic BLT sandwich, serve with a dollop of aioli (see page 138) or mayonnaise. Squeeze a little lime or lemon juice to keep the brilliant green colour of your avocado from turning brown.

seared scallop & watercress salad

hoisin chicken

Seared Scallop & Watercress Salad

1	small celery root, peeled and quartered
2	cups chicken stock
2	cups water
1	tablespoon unsalted butter
¼	cup 35% cream
2	Italian sausages, cooked and kept warm
12	sea scallops
2	tablespoons clarified butter
¼	cup watercress mustard oil (see page 141)

1. Place celery root in a small saucepan and cover with chicken stock and water. Bring to a boil and simmer until soft. This should take approximately 20-30 minutes.
2. In a blender, purée celery root and remaining liquid until smooth. Drop in butter and cream. Blend until combined.
3. Heat a large sauté pan over medium-high heat. Add clarified butter and place scallops in the pan. Cook for 2 minutes until scallops develop a golden colour. Gently turn each scallop over and cook for 2 more minutes. Set aside.
4. Slice sausage in half lengthwise and each half in two.
5. Place a ¼ cup of celery root purée in the middle of plate, lay 2 pieces of sausage in the purée and top with some watercress. Place 3 scallops in and around watercress and drizzle with watercress mustard oil. **SERVES 4**

Nutrients per serving: 391 calories, 27 g protein, 3 g fibre, 25 g fat, 14 g carbohydrates. Excellent source of vitamins A and B$_{12}$.

Hoisin Chicken

2	cups hoisin
2	tablespoons sambal oelek
2	bunches green onions, chopped
1	cup red wine
6	cloves garlic, smashed
1	3-inch piece ginger, peeled and sliced
8	boneless chicken breasts

1. Combine all ingredients except chicken in a bowl and mix. Add chicken and marinate for at least 4 hours or overnight.
2. Remove chicken and discard remaining marinade.
3. Grill over medium heat on the barbecue or bake in a 400 F oven until chicken is done (about 15-20 minutes).
4. Serve with a bowl of white or brown rice. **SERVES 8**

Nutrients per serving: 482 calories, 27 g protein, 12 g fat, 63 g carbohydrates, 1 g fibre. Excellent source of niacin, vitamin B$_6$, pantothenic acid and zinc.

cooking 101
phyllo pastry

equipment

sauté pan
cutting board
pastry brush
parchment paper
baking sheet

ingredients

2   Yukon Gold potatoes, peeled and cut into ¼-inch cubes, parboiled
2   tablespoons unsalted butter
2   tablespoons olive oil
1   cup finely diced onion
1   clove garlic, minced
3   cups sliced button mushrooms
2   cups sliced shiitake mushrooms
2   tablespoons white wine
6   ounces goat cheese, crumbled
2   tablespoons finely chopped fresh oregano
2   tablespoons finely chopped fresh thyme
2   tablespoons finely chopped fresh Italian parsley
1   package phyllo dough, defrosted
½   cup melted clarified butter

Wild Mushroom Strudel

Mushroom Filling

1. Melt 1 tablespoon of butter with 1 tablespoon of olive oil in a large sauté pan over medium heat. Cook onion and garlic until soft, then add button mushrooms and sauté until lightly browned. Add this mixture to the parboiled potatoes.

2. Melt remaining butter and olive oil in the same sauté pan and cook shiitake mushrooms until golden. Add shiitakes to potato mixture. Deglaze sauté pan with white wine and add to potato mushroom mixture. Gently mix in goat cheese and herbs. Season with salt and pepper.

Working With Phyllo

3. Preheat oven to 400 F.

4. Lay one sheet of phyllo on a clean, dry surface and brush with a small amount of clarified butter. Continue layering with two more sheets of phyllo, brushing each sheet with clarified butter.

5. Place mushroom mixture across lower third of phyllo layers. Roll up the phyllo, tucking in sides to seal in mixture, and place on a parchment-lined baking tray. Brush the outside of strudel with clarified butter and refrigerate for 30 minutes.

6. Bake for 20 minutes, rotate tray and lower the heat to 350 F, and bake for 20 more minutes until golden brown. **SERVES 6**

Nutrients per serving: 382 calories, 30 g fat, 7 g protein, 24 g carbohydrates, 4 g fibre. High source of fibre. Excellent source of vitamin D, pantothenic acid, riboflavin and zinc.

wild mushroom strudel

grilled steak
baguette sandwich

rosemary roasted
yukon gold potatoes

Grilled Steak Baguette Sandwich

¼   cup olive oil
3   sprigs fresh rosemary, picked and chopped
2   teaspoons chopped fresh Italian parsley
2   teaspoons picked fresh thyme
2   cloves garlic, minced
1   tablespoon kosher salt
1   tablespoon cracked black pepper
1   7-ounce striploin steak, trimmed
6   tablespoons red onion marmalade (see page 140)
1   baguette, cut in half for 2 sandwiches

1. Combine olive oil, rosemary, parsley, thyme, garlic, salt and pepper. Rub steak with herb mixture and grill to medium rare.
2. Spread half red onion marmalade on bottom halves of bread. Slice and divvy up steak. Top with remaining marmalade. Close the sandwich and dig in. **SERVES 2**

Nutrients per serving: 989 calories, 47 g fat, 40 g protein, 97 g carbohydrates, 6 g fibre. Excellent source of vitamins B$_6$, B$_{12}$ and E, folate, niacin, thiamin, riboflavin, iron, zinc, phosphorus and magnesium.

Rosemary Roasted Yukon Gold Potatoes

12   Yukon Gold potatoes, sliced into ½-inch rounds (peeling optional)
½   cup clarified butter, melted
4   cloves garlic, minced
2   tablespoons fresh rosemary leaves
2   teaspoons salt

1. Preheat oven to 425 F. Place a baking sheet in the oven to heat up.
2. Place potatoes in a large pot with enough cold, salted water to cover. Bring to a boil, lower heat and simmer for 5 minutes. Drain potatoes and place back into pot. Toss to roughen edges and let dry for 2 minutes. Coat with clarified butter.
3. Spread potatoes out on baking sheet. Bake for 35-40 minutes, turning potatoes halfway through cooking time.
4. Sprinkle with garlic, rosemary and salt, and continue cooking for an additional 15 minutes. **SERVES 8**

Nutrients per serving: 285 calories, 3.5 g protein, 13 g fat, 40 g carbohydrates, 2 g fibre. Excellent source of vitamin B$_6$.

Roast Goose

1   8- to 10-pound goose
2   white onions, cut into quarters
1   leek, cut into ½-inch pieces
3   carrots, cut into ½-inch pieces
1   bunch fresh thyme
½   bunch fresh rosemary

1. Preheat oven to 475 F.
2. Remove giblets from goose. Rinse and pat dry. Pinch skin and randomly poke 8-10 holes without piercing the meat. Lay the goose breast-side down on a roasting rack and place in roasting pan.
3. Pour ½ inch of boiling water into the bottom of pan and cover. If you don't have a roasting pan with a lid, cover loosely with aluminum foil. Carefully transfer roasting pan to oven and steam goose for 1 hour.
4. Reduce temperature to 400 F. Remove lid from roasting pan and lay vegetables and herbs at bottom. Roast goose for approximately 1 hour, and baste every 20 minutes with the juices from the pan.
5. For last 15 minutes of roasting time, turn the goose over to allow the skin to crisp and develop a golden colour.
SERVES 8

Nutrients per serving: 1,210 calories, 107 g fat, 51 g protein, 8 g carbohydrates, 2 g fibre. Excellent source of vitamins A, B$_6$, B$_{12}$ and E, niacin, riboflavin, pantothenic acid, iron, zinc, phosphorus and magnesium. Good source of folate, vitamin C and thiamin.

Chef's tip: Allow meat to rest before carving. Then lightly sprinkle slices with salt for the best flavour.
Carving note: Unlike chicken or turkey, the legs (not the breasts) are the meatiest sections of the goose.

roast goose

market vegetable salad

pasta e fagioli

italian wedding soup

Market Vegetable Salad

1	tablespoon grainy mustard
2	tablespoons sesame oil
¼	cup white-wine vinegar
2	tablespoons rice vinegar
½	cup grapeseed oil
1	red pepper, julienned
1	yellow pepper, julienned
½	pound green beans, trimmed and blanched
1	bunch carrots with tops, peeled and blanched
½	pound sugar snap peas, blanched
1	head broccoli florets, stems trimmed and blanched
1	teaspoon sea salt

1. Place grainy mustard and sesame oil in a small bowl. Whisk in vinegars. Slowly pour in grapeseed oil, whisking to emulsify.
2. Toss dressing with vegetables and season with salt.
SERVES 6

Nutrients per serving: 308 calories, 25 g fat, 6 g protein, 20 g carbohydrates, 5 g fibre. Excellent source of fibre, vitamins A and C, folate and magnesium. Good source of vitamin B_6.

Chef's tip: Deep-coloured vegetables are packed with anti-oxidants and dietary fibre. Customize this recipe to your own taste with the freshest vegetables available.

Pasta e Fagioli

2	cups dried romano or cranberry beans
3	tablespoons olive oil
1	28-ounce can plum tomatoes
2	cloves garlic, smashed
1	celery stalk, cut in half
3	stems of fresh basil
3	stems of fresh Italian parsley
2	cups tubetti pasta, cooked al dente
1	bunch green onions, chopped
1	cup grated Parmesan
	salt and pepper to taste

1. Cover beans in cold water and soak overnight.
2. Heat olive oil in a large pot. Add garlic and tomatoes and cook for 5 minutes over medium heat. Add drained beans, 6 cups of water, celery, basil and parsley. Bring to a boil, reduce heat and simmer until beans are soft.
3. Remove celery, basil, parsley and garlic. Add pasta, salt, pepper, and heat through. Garnish with green onions and Parmesan. **SERVES 8**

Nutrients per serving: 274 calories, 10 g fat, 10 g protein, 38 g carbohydrates, 7 g fibre. Excellent source of fibre.

moroccan quinoa salad

cooking 101: quinoa

This three-step cooking process produces a nice fluffy grain that is perfect for this salad.

Use a 4-quart saucepan that accommodates a steamer insert.

1. RINSE. Rinse quinoa with water.

2. BOIL. Bring a large pot of salted water to a boil and cook quinoa for 10 minutes. Drain into a colander and rinse with cold water.

3. STEAM. In the same pot, bring 1¼ inches of water to a boil. Transfer quinoa to cheesecloth-lined steamer.

Cover steamer with a tight lid. Steam for 10 minutes or until tender and fluffy.

Chef's tip: Line a simple vegetable steamer with a basket-style coffee filter.

SHORTCUT. Rinse quinoa in cold water. Bring 2 cups salted water to a boil. Add quinoa and bring back to a boil. Reduce heat and simmer until most water has evaporated (15-18 minutes). Rest 5 minutes, then fluff.

Italian Wedding Soup

1	whole celery heart, finely chopped
1	teaspoon olive oil
2	eggs
¼	cup milk
1	loaf white Italian bread cut into ½- inch croutons (air-dried one day before)
6	cups chicken stock
36	cooked mini veal meatballs (see page 139)
¼	cup fresh Italian parsley, chopped
½	cup grated Parmesan

1. Sweat celery in olive oil over medium heat until translucent. Set aside.
2. Whisk eggs and milk together. Toss croutons in egg/milk mixture. Fry croutons in a 10-inch sauté pan in ¼ inch of olive oil. Drain on paper towels and set aside.
3. In six shallow soup bowls, divide celery, croutons and meatballs, and ladle in 6-8 ounces hot chicken broth. Sprinkle each with 1 teaspoon parsley and 1 tablespoon Parmesan. **SERVES 6**

Nutrients per serving: 366 calories, 19 g fat, 31 g protein, 14 g carbohydrates, 2 g fibre.

Moroccan Quinoa Salad

1	cup quinoa
⅓	cup fresh lemon juice
3	tablespoons olive oil
2	teaspoons ground cumin
1	teaspoon salt
¼	teaspoon granulated sugar
1½	cups canned black beans, rinsed
1½	cups cooked corn kernels
½	small red onion, thinly sliced
1	pint cherry tomatoes, quartered
½	cup slivered almonds, toasted
¼	cup chopped green or black olives
¼	cup chopped fresh mint
¼	cup chopped fresh coriander

1. Cook quinoa. While quinoa is cooking, whisk together lemon juice, olive oil, cumin, salt and sugar into a vinaigrette in a small bowl. Combine quinoa and all remaining ingredients, except fresh herbs, into a medium-sized bowl.
2. Drizzle with vinaigrette and toss to combine.
3. Refrigerate for at least one hour to allow flavours to combine. Add fresh herbs just prior to serving. May be served at room temperature. **SERVES 8**

Nutrients per serving: 407 calories, 17 g fat, 14 g protein, 56 g carbohydrates, 11 g fibre. Excellent source of vitamin E, folic acid, thiamin, iron, zinc, phosphorus and magnesium.

sunday supper

Revive and update an old tradition. Return to the Sunday dinner table
with good friends, great food ideas and a modern sense of occasion.
It doesn't have to be fussy – simple often works best.

the menu
arctic char
warm potato salad
corn on the cob
cupcakes to go

69

creating a sense of occasion

Set a scene that will make the meal feel special. A few steps can create a beautiful ambience.

☐ **Set the Table** For an eclectic mix of casual and formal, use everyday plates and pair them with your best linen napkins, wine and water glasses.

☐ **Add Flowers** A bold hit of colour makes a huge impact. Stick to one type of flower in no more than three shades. Keep the arrangements low so you can see your guests across the table.

☐ **Make an Entrance** Salt-baked char makes a statement and adds a sense of ceremony when presented on a large wooden tray.

☐ **The Extra Mile** Finish each setting with a gift box so guests can take a little bit of the evening home. Simple grosgrain ribbons layer together to make a classic, white gift box special.

Salt-Baked Arctic Char

This fish is almost impossible to overcook – and the salt crust ensures it won't dry out.

1	3-pound Arctic char, cleaned
1	sprig fresh rosemary
¼	bunch fresh chives
4	sprigs fresh Italian parsley
1	lemon, sliced
3	egg whites
¼	cup cold water
1	3-pound box kosher salt
	Béarnaise sauce (see page 138)

1. Preheat oven to 400 F.
2. Rinse char under cold water and pat dry. Stuff rosemary, chives, parsley and lemon slices into cavity of fish.
3. Whisk together egg whites and water. Add salt and mix well. Spread 3 cups of salt mixture along bottom of baking sheet. This layer should be large enough to fit outline of fish. Place fish on top. Completely cover with a ½-inch layer of salt mixture.
4. Bake for 25 minutes or until an internal temperature of 140 F is reached. (Allowing the fish to cool inside the crust will keep it moist, even if you don't serve it right away.)
5. When ready to serve, crack through salt with a rolling pin, peel back skin and serve with warm Béarnaise sauce.
SERVES 6 TO 8

salt-baked arctic char

warm potato salad with arctic char

steamed corn

Warm Potato Salad

This light, flavourful salad can be kept in the refrigerator for up to three days. Great for a midnight snack.

3   pounds red-skinned new potatoes, cut in half
¼   cup grainy Dijon mustard
¼   cup white-wine vinegar
½   cup extra-virgin olive oil
1   medium red onion, finely chopped
½   bunch fresh chives, finely chopped
1   tablespoon sea salt
2   teaspoons cracked black pepper

1. Mix together mustard, vinegar and olive oil.
2. Place potatoes in large pot of well-salted, cold water. Bring to a boil and reduce heat immediately. Simmer until tender. Drain and spread potatoes on a baking sheet. Allow them to steam dry.
3. Toss warm potatoes with vinaigrette. Add remaining ingredients and serve immediately. **SERVES 6**

Steamed Corn on the Cob
To create a stunning visual effect, as well as a nifty holder for the cob, pull the outer husks back, leaving them attached, and tie with butcher's twine. Cut off the pointed end of the cob. Lay a steamer basket inside a tall pot filled with 3 inches of water. Bring water to a boil. Stand cobs in the pot, cut-end down. Cover with aluminum foil and steam for 8 minutes. Serve hot with herb butter, coarse salt and fresh cracked pepper.

Quick Herb Butter
Take 1 pound of unsalted butter and soften to room temperature. Mix 4 tablespoons of pesto into butter. Shape butter in wax paper into a 2-inch thick log. Refrigerate and keep on hand for flavouring corn, or for topping grilled steaks, fish and vegetables.

Dessert-to-Go
Fill gift boxes with homemade goodies. Or to save time, order extra cupcakes or cookies from your favourite bakery. That way, you can all enjoy dessert, and your guests will also go home with a sweet memory of the evening.

wine gathering

The long-awaited release of Beaujolais Nouveau is a great excuse to throw a party. Create a warm, casual feel for this late-autumn harvest celebration with a selection of great cheeses and a fabulous noshing menu.

beaujolais
nouveau

*tasting
menu*

spiced olives, pâtés & nuts
cheese board
wild mushroom soup
fennel tapenade & flatbread

new brunswick
sheep's milk cheese

perfect pairings

☐ **Special Welcome** Even the smallest gathering
feels special with a custom-made invitation.
Create a wine-tasting journal to catalogue
labels and record tasting notes. It's a great gift,
and can be used to remember your favourite
wines all year.

☐ **The Room** An intimate space will make guests
want to linger. Floor cushions are ideal for
sitting around the coffee table. Pull out lots of
throw pillows and blankets to curl up on. Light
a fire and plenty of candles.

☐ **The Ambience** Load up the stereo with a variety
of your favourite music, push the random
button, and sit back and enjoy.

☐ **The Lighting** Use unscented candles around
food and wine. Strong scents can affect your
tasting experience.

nouveau wine

Beaujolais Nouveau is released on the third Thursday of
November every year. The tradition began in France, where
people use the occasion to celebrate the end of harvest.

Taste. Expect an unsophisticated, fruity "new wine,"
low in tannins.

Varietal. The grape for Beaujolais Nouveau is Gamay.

Process. Carbonic Maceration is a sort of winemaking
shortcut, so the wine can be made and released
almost immediately.

Geography. All the grapes in the Beaujolais region must
be picked by hand. These are the only vineyards, along
with Champagne, where hand-harvesting is mandatory
in France.

Aging. Nouveaus are meant to be enjoyed young. They
should ideally be consumed by May of the year following
their release.

Temperature. Serve Nouveaus slightly cool, at about 12 C.

Beyond France. Wine producers around the world have
now joined the tradition. When you visit your local wine
store in November, you might also find Nouveaus from
California or Canada and Novellos from Italy.

wild rice &
mushroom soup
(see page 87)

Fennel Tapenade

Serve with a selection of breads and crackers. Leftovers make an excellent sandwich spread.

1	medium fennel bulb, cut vertically into 6 pieces
¼	cup pine nuts, toasted
½	cup green olives with pimento
1	teaspoon capers
1	tablespoon chopped fresh Italian parsley
6	cloves garlic, roasted
	zest of one lemon
½	cup fennel fronds

1. Preheat oven to 350 F.
2. Brush fennel pieces with oil and lay on a parchment-lined baking sheet. Season with salt and pepper.
3. Roast until soft, about 30-40 minutes.
4. Place fennel with remaining ingredients into bowl of a food processor and pulse until well combined.
MAKES 1½ CUPS

Baked Brie in Phyllo Pastry

Prepare the day before and pop in the oven half an hour before guests arrive.

1	8-inch brie wheel
1	package phyllo dough
½	cup melted clarified butter
2	tablespoons finely chopped rosemary

1. Preheat oven to 375 F.
2. Unwrap phyllo dough carefully to avoid tears and cover with a damp kitchen towel. Place 1 sheet on a clean, dry surface. Brush entire surface with some clarified butter.
3. Lay another sheet on top and brush with clarified butter. Repeat two more times.
4. Lay brie in the centre of stacked, buttered phyllo sheets. Bring edges of phyllo up and around to enclose entire wheel, making a sealed package. Brush outside of package with clarified butter.
5. Place brie on a parchment-lined baking sheet and refrigerate for a minimum of 45 minutes.
6. Bake for 25 minutes.
SERVES 8 TO 10

baked brie in phyllo pastry

market fresh this season

blood oranges

chestnuts

collard greens

florida oranges

grapefruit

jerusalem artichoke

meyer lemons

mussels

persimmons

pomegranate

pomelo

tangerines

winter

wild rice & barley
oatmeal with dried fruit

smoked salmon
eggs benedict

Wild Rice & Barley Oatmeal with Dried Fruit

½ cup wild rice
½ cup pearl barley
½ cup Irish oats
¼ cup brown sugar, firmly packed
1½ tablespoons butter
1 teaspoon salt
½ teaspoon ground cinnamon
½ teaspoon allspice
½ cup sliced dried apricots
½ cup dried cranberries

1. Preheat oven to 375 F.
2. In a small saucepan, simmer wild rice in 2 cups water for 20 minutes. Drain.
3. In a large bowl, gently mix together pearl barley, Irish oats, brown sugar, butter, salt, ground cinnamon, allspice, the cooked wild rice and 6 cups water. Pour into a 2½-quart non-stick baking dish, cover loosely with aluminum foil and bake for approximately 1½ hours. Remove from oven and stir in sliced dried apricots and dried cranberries. **SERVES 6**

Nutrients per serving: 277 calories, 3 g fat, 7 g protein, 59 g carbohydrates, 5 g fibre. High source of fibre. Excellent source of magnesium. Good source of iron, zinc and phosphorus.

Smoked Salmon Eggs Benedict

4 croissants
8 poached eggs
4 slices smoked salmon
1 cup Béarnaise sauce (see page 138)

1. Slice croissants in half horizontally. Place cut-side down on a baking sheet and warm in a 200 F oven for 5 minutes.
2. Place the bottom half of each croissant on a plate and lay a piece of smoked salmon on top. Nestle 2 poached eggs on top of salmon. Spoon a generous amount of Béarnaise sauce over eggs. Top with remaining croissant half.
SERVES 4

Nutrients per serving: 563 calories, 22 g protein, 40 g fat, 28 g carbohydrates, 2 g fibre. Excellent source of vitamins A and B_{12}.

Marinated Lamb Roast

1 4-pound boneless leg of lamb
2 teaspoons kosher salt
1 teaspoon cracked black pepper
chermoula marinade (see page 138)

1. Preheat oven to 425 F.
2. Open leg of lamb and gently pound meat to even out the thickness. Rub meat with chermoula marinade.
3. Cut three 15-inch pieces of butcher's twine. Roll meat tightly into a log and, with seam-side down, wrap twine around the centre and tie. Tie the remaining twine around each end. Place lamb in the refrigerator for a minimum of 2 hours or overnight to allow flavours to penetrate the meat.
4. Remove lamb from fridge and allow to come back to room temperature before roasting. Season lamb with salt and pepper, and place on a rack in a roasting pan or on a baking sheet. Roast until the internal temperature reaches 140 F (approximately 1-1¼ hours) for medium doneness. After removing roast from oven, allow to rest for 10 minutes before slicing. **SERVES 6**

Nutrients per serving: 554 calories, 55 g protein, 35 g fat, 4 g carbohydrates, 2 g fibre. Excellent source of riboflavin, iron and vitamin B_{12}.

marinated
lamb roast

oven-roasted tomatoes

smoked mackerel pâté

Oven-Roasted Tomatoes

12	Roma tomatoes
2	tablespoons extra-virgin olive oil
½	cup chopped fresh thyme
2	tablespoons sea salt

1. Preheat oven to 250 F.
2. Cut tomatoes lengthwise and lay flesh-side up on a cooling rack. Place rack on a baking sheet lined with parchment paper. Drizzle each tomato with ½ teaspoon of extra-virgin olive oil and sprinkle with thyme and salt.
3. Roast for approximately 2½ hours. Remove from oven. The tomatoes will begin to pucker, but will still be moist. Oven-roasted tomatoes may be stored for several days in the fridge in an airtight container.

Nutrients per 1 tomato: 34 calories, 1 g fat, 1 g protein, 6 g carbohydrates, 2 g fibre.

Smoked Mackerel Pâté

8	ounces cream cheese
8	ounces smoked mackerel, skin removed, broken into pieces
1	teaspoon cayenne pepper
2	tablespoons fresh lemon juice

1. Place all ingredients in a food processor and mix until well combined. Chill for 30 minutes and serve with your favourite crackers or flatbreads. **MAKES 2 CUPS**

Nutrients per serving: 173 calories, 9 g protein, 15 g fat, 1 g carbohydrates.

wild rice & mushroom soup

Wild Rice & Mushroom Soup

½	cup wild rice
4	teaspoons salt
1½	cups cold water
¼	cup unsalted butter
1	cup sliced button mushrooms
2½	cups torn oyster mushrooms
2½	cups sliced shiitake mushroom caps
½	cup finely chopped shallots
1	celery stalk, finely chopped
2	tablespoons minced garlic
⅓	cup brandy
2	tablespoons all-purpose flour
7	cups warm mushroom stock (see page 140)
1	tablespoon chopped fresh thyme
1	pinch nutmeg
½	cup 35% cream

1. Place wild rice, salt and water in a small pot and bring to a boil. Reduce heat to medium and cook for 30 to 35 minutes, until the rice is soft and grains are slightly bursting. Drain and set aside.
2. Melt 2 tablespoons of butter in a large pot and cook each type of mushroom separately until soft and golden, about 3 minutes. Add more butter to your pot if necessary. Remove mushrooms and set aside.

3. Add shallots, celery and garlic to pot and cook until soft, about 5 minutes. Add brandy and deglaze pan, scraping any browned bits from the bottom.
4. Add flour and stir for 1 minute. Slowly pour in mushroom stock, whisking constantly to prevent lumps. Simmer for 20 minutes, stirring occasionally.
5. Add thyme, nutmeg and cream. Stir in reserved mushrooms and wild rice. Season with salt and pepper.
6. Reheat over medium heat. Excess heat may cause soup to separate. **SERVES 6**

Nutrients per serving: *325 calories, 16 g fat, 9 g protein, 29 g carbohydrates, 4 g fibre. High source of fibre. Excellent source of vitamin D, folate, riboflavin, pantothenic acid and zinc.*

dry herbs

Buying: Purchase in small amounts and well-sealed packages.

Storing: Store in a cool, dry place with minimum exposure to light. Don't store herbs above the stove, as the heat will diminish their taste. Label the container with the purchase date, and use within one year. Don't freeze your dried herbs, because the slightest moisture will dissipate the flavour. **Chef's tip:** Test the freshness of dried herbs by pinching a little with your fingertips and rubbing. If there's no aroma, it's ready for the compost.

Cooking: Best added at the start of cooking, as heat is needed to bring out flavour. Great for making dry rubs and marinades.
Chef's tip: Before you add dry herbs, wake them up by rubbing them in the palm of your hand with a pinch of coarse salt.

Convert
If you're substituting dry for fresh herbs, here's a helpful conversion:
1 tablespoon fresh = 1 teaspoon dried

soda bread
cooking 101

1. Preheat oven to 350 F. Whisk together buttermilk and egg in a small bowl. In a larger bowl, combine all dry ingredients. Using your hands, mix butter into the dry ingredients until it resembles cornmeal.

2. Pour wet ingredients into dry.

3. Combine ingredients together until the dough forms a ball.

4. Turn the dough out onto a lightly floured surface and knead for 5 minutes until soft and elastic.

equipment

mixing bowls
measuring cups
whisk
knife
baking sheet
parchment paper

ingredients

1½   cups buttermilk
1   egg
2   cups whole wheat flour
1½   cups all-purpose flour
½   cup old-fashioned rolled oats
2   tablespoons brown sugar
2   teaspoons salt
1   teaspoon baking soda
1   teaspoon baking powder
3   tablespoons unsalted butter, cold

5. Shape into a round loaf approximately 6 inches in diameter. Dust top with a little flour and, with a sharp knife, cut a large X into the top, half the depth of the loaf and to within one inch of the edge. Place on a parchment-lined baking sheet and bake for 45-50 minutes.

6. As the loaf bakes, it opens up. It should sound hollow when you tap the bottom.

soda bread

turkey breast
with shiitake
mushroom stuffing

cranberry jam

Turkey Breast with Shiitake Mushroom Stuffing

2	turkey breasts, boneless, skin on (1 1/2 pounds each)
2 1/2	cups sliced shiitake mushrooms
2	tablespoons olive oil
2	tablespoons finely chopped shallots
1	tablespoon finely chopped garlic
1/4	cup sherry
2	teaspoons salt
1	teaspoon pepper
1/2	cup sautéed Swiss chard, chopped
3/4	cup 35% cream
1/4	cup chopped fresh chives
1	lemon, zested

1. Preheat oven to 375 F. Remove the tenderloins from breasts and set aside.
2. In a medium sauté pan, cook mushrooms in olive oil for 2-3 minutes over medium-high heat. Add shallots, garlic, 1 teaspoon salt and 1/2 teaspoon pepper and cook for another 2 minutes. Deglaze with sherry. Remove from pan and let cool.
3. Place turkey tenderloins into food processor and pulse with cream and remaining salt and pepper. Add mushrooms, Swiss chard and lemon zest. Pulse until well combined. Remove from food processor and mix in chopped chives.
4. Cut a pocket into thickest part of each turkey breast and fill with 1/2 cup of filling. Close pocket. Tuck thinner end of breast under. Tie breast in three spots, starting at the smallest end. This will create a rolled turkey breast and ensure even cooking.
5. Drizzle breasts with a little olive oil. Heat a large, oven-proof sauté pan over high heat. Place breast skin-side down and sear for 5 minutes or until golden. Flip over and place pan in oven for 30 minutes or until internal temperature reads 165 F. Let breasts rest for 10 minutes. Slice and serve. **SERVES 6**

Nutrients per serving: *402 calories, 24 g fat, 34 g protein, 10 g carbohydrates, 1 g fibre. Excellent source of vitamins B_6, B_{12} and D, niacin, zinc and phosphorus. Good source of vitamins A and E, riboflavin, iron and magnesium.*

Spinach Crepe Manicotti

1	8-ounce bag spinach, cooked, drained and roughly chopped
1	475 ml tub ricotta cheese
1	egg
1/2	cup grated mozzarella
2	tablespoons chopped fresh parsley
2	tablespoons chopped fresh basil
3	tablespoons grated Parmesan
3	cups tomato sauce
12	crepes

1. Preheat oven to 350F.
2. Mix all ingredients, except tomato sauce and crepes, until well combined.
3. Lay out a crepe and fill with 2 tablespoons of mixture. Roll crepe to enclose mixture. Continue with remaining crepes.
4. Ladle 1/2 cup of tomato sauce into an 11" x 9" baking dish, lay crepes in and cover with remaining tomato sauce. Bake for 15 minutes or until filling is hot. **SERVES 6**

Nutrients per serving: *419 calories, 18 g fat, 30 g protein, 35 g carbohydrates, 5 g fibre.*

Cranberry Jam

1	orange
2	cups cranberries, fresh or frozen
1	Bartlett pear, peeled and cubed
1	package Certo crystals
2	cups granulated sugar

1. Zest and segment orange, keeping all juice.
2. Place zest, segments and juice in a medium saucepan. Add cranberries, pears and Certo. Bring to a boil. Add sugar and continue to boil while constantly stirring for 2 minutes. Cool completely. **MAKES 4 CUPS**

spinach
crepe manicotti

spicy korean chicken pot

chili pickled mushrooms

Spicy Korean Chicken Pot

2	tablespoons vegetable oil
2	chicken drumsticks
2	chicken thighs
2	chicken breasts
4	potatoes, peeled and cut into 1-inch pieces
4	carrots, peeled and cut into 1-inch pieces
1	large onion, cut into 1-inch pieces
2	tablespoons Korean spicy paste
1	tablespoon Korean chili powder
1	tablespoon honey
1	cup chicken stock or water

1. Heat vegetable oil in a large pan over medium heat. Sear chicken pieces in batches to allow even browning. Remove and set aside. In the same pan, add vegetables and cook until onion is translucent. Season with salt and pepper.
2. Return the chicken pieces to the pan and add the spicy paste, chili powder, honey and chicken stock.
3. Bring to a boil, stir, then simmer covered for 45 minutes. Serve with white rice. **SERVES 6**

Nutrients per serving: 435 calories, 20 g fat, 29 g protein, 37 g carbohydrates, 5 g fibre.

Chef's tip: If you can't find Korean spices at an Asian grocery store, use hot paprika or regular chili pepper.

Chili Pickled Mushrooms

1	cup tarragon vinegar
1	cup water
1	teaspoon coriander seeds
1	teaspoon fennel seeds
1	teaspoon mustard seeds
1	tablespoon black peppercorns
2	bay leaves
1	teaspoon red chili flakes
1	pound button mushrooms, stems trimmed

1. Place all ingredients except mushrooms into a stainless-steel pot and bring to a boil. Add mushrooms and stir.
2. Turn off heat, let stand for 5 minutes. Transfer mushrooms to a glass jar or ceramic container and cover with remaining cooking liquid. Store in refrigerator for up to 2 weeks. **MAKES 6 CUPS**

Nutrients per ¼ cup serving: 7 calories, 0 g fat, 1 g protein, 1 g carbohydrates.

miso soup

roasted sesame chickpeas

Miso Soup

8	cups dashi stock (see page 139)
3	tablespoons miso paste
1	cup soy sauce
1	cup cubed semi-firm tofu
	seaweed garnish

1. Gently heat dashi in a medium saucepan, then add miso paste and soy sauce.

2. Divide tofu into 8 bowls and place a little seaweed garnish on top. Pour soup into bowls. **SERVES 8**

Nutrients per serving: *47 calories, 3.3 g protein, 0.6 g fat, 8.1 g carbohydrates, 1.2 g fibre. Good source of magnesium.*

Chef's tip: Japanese restaurants often come up with signature garnishes for their miso. Try adding or mixing to make your own: sliced green onions, soba noodles, daikon sprouts, shrimp.

Roasted Sesame Chickpeas

1	cup dried or canned chickpeas
1	teaspoon soy sauce
1	teaspoon sesame oil
1	teaspoon chili powder

1. Rinse 1 cup of dried chickpeas and cover with water. Allow them to soak overnight, then drain. (If using canned, rinse, drain and pat dry.)

2. Spread on a baking sheet and roast at 400 F for 30 minutes or until tender.

3. Remove from oven and toss with seasonings.

Nutrients per ¼ cup serving: *197 calories, 9 g protein, 6 g fat, 28 g carbohydrates, 4 g fibre. Excellent source of folic acid.*

Chef's tip: Substitute other oils, herbs or spices. One of our other favourites is olive oil, salt and lemon zest.

new year's

in the bag

Ring in the year by ordering in the magic of India. And set the scene with warm light, lush colours and fragrant petals. Get inspired by takeout menus from around the world and add new life (and ease) to the party.

what to order
Variety is the spice of life. Indian takeout offers flavours for any palate: mild to spicy, vegetarian, salty or sweet – and there is always a vast selection of seafoods and meats.

1. Samosa
Crispy triangular pastry filled with potatoes, green peas and spices.

2. Shrimp Tikka
Shrimp marinated in yogurt and spices, and cooked in a tandoor oven.

3. Chana Masala
Chickpeas cooked with aromatic spices and a touch of mint.

4. Aloo Ghobi
Lightly spiced cauliflower and potatoes cooked with tomatoes and onions.

5. Lamb Vindaloo
Boneless lamb and potatoes simmered in a fiery, tangy sauce.

6. Butter Chicken
Tandoori chicken cooked in a creamy tomato sauce.

7. Dahl
Lentils simmered with ginger, cumin and garlic.

the sides
Essential to the meal are the traditional Indian condiments and, of course, basmati rice.

A. Pappadums
Crispy cumin-spiced flat crackers.

B. Mango Pickle
Savoury and sour with a hint of spice. A little goes a long way with this condiment.

C. Raita
A cucumber and yogurt sauce that cools the palate.

D. Basmati Rice Pilaf
Scented with cardamom and curry leaves.

E. Naan
Unleavened bread traditionally cooked in a tandoor oven.

F. Mango Chutney
A thick, sweet relish-like condiment to balance out your spicy meal.

kulfi

paan

setting the mood

☐ **Take a trip to Little India** (or any store that imports exotic home accessories).

☐ **Hang brightly coloured saris** or fabric from wires strung around the table, and envelop the room in deep hues of orange and pink.

☐ **Embellish the table** with ornate glass votive candles and surround them with a light blanket of multi-coloured rose petals.

☐ **Bunches of shimmering children's bangles** make perfect napkin rings.

☐ **Small jewelled boxes** or other inexpensive knick-knacks make lovely table favours and keepsakes.

entertaining secrets When ordering in, check beforehand to make sure your favourite takeout restaurant is open during the holidays. To make it seamless, pre-order a few days before the party. Never fret about being short on chairs, rent them instead. You can also rent tables, dishes, whatever you need. And the best part of renting dishes – no washing up.

flower power To add a personal touch, garnish your dishes with edible flowers, curry leaves and fresh herbs.

festive drinks Match the beverage to the menu. For an Indian meal, beer, white wine and sparkling wine are the drinks of choice. They'll cool the palate for the spicy dishes. Imported beers, like Kingfisher from India, are easy to find and will contribute to the authentic feel of the evening.

sweet ending Kulfi (ice cream) and paan (a betel palm leaf wrapped around betel nuts and lime) are quintessential Indian desserts and easy to purchase pre-made.

sweets

raspberry &
strawberry granita

cranberry yogurt muffins

Raspberry & Strawberry Granita

¾ cup granulated sugar
1 cup water
1 cup fresh lemon juice
1 cup strawberry juice
1 pint fresh raspberries, crushed with a fork

1. Combine sugar, water and juices in a saucepan and cook over medium heat, stirring until sugar is dissolved. Let cool.
2. Pour cooled mixture into a shallow pan, add crushed raspberries and stir. Place in freezer for one hour.
3. Remove from freezer and fork the crystals that have formed around the edges into the rest of the juice. Continue to do this at intervals for another hour, forking the slush to break it up as it freezes. The result is fine shards of ice.
SERVES 6

Nutrients per serving: 151 calories, 0 g fat, 1 g protein, 40 g carbohydrates, 2 g fibre. Excellent source of vitamin C.

Chef's tip: Put serving glasses in the freezer in the afternoon. A frosted glass will help keep the granita cold.

Cranberry Yogurt Muffins

2 cups all-purpose flour
¾ cup rolled oats
1 cup granulated sugar
½ teaspoon baking soda
¾ teaspoon baking powder
½ teaspoon salt
1 teaspoon ground ginger
2 eggs
¾ cup plain yogurt
¼ cup vegetable oil
1 teaspoon vanilla extract
1½ cups cranberries – fresh or frozen, chopped in food processor
1 Granny Smith apple, grated

1. Preheat oven to 375 F.
2. Combine dry ingredients in a bowl. In a separate bowl, combine eggs, yogurt, vegetable oil and vanilla extract.
3. Mix wet ingredients into dry, then add cranberries and apple. Use a spoon or an ice cream scoop to drop mix into a non-stick muffin tin. Fill to the top.
4. Bake for 30 minutes until golden. **MAKES 1 DOZEN**

Nutrients per serving: 237 calories, 6 g fat, 5 g protein, 41 g carbohydrates, 2 g fibre. Excellent source of vitamin D. Good source of folic acid.

Dutch Chocolate Cake

1 cup granulated sugar
1 cup all-purpose flour
1 teaspoon baking soda
½ teaspoon baking powder
¼ teaspoon salt
3 tablespoons cocoa powder
½ cup water
½ cup milk
¼ cup vegetable oil
1 egg, lightly beaten
½ teaspoon vanilla
1 cup 35% cream, whipped to soft peaks
raspberry sauce (see page 140)

1. Preheat oven to 350 F.
2. Sift together all dry ingredients, except cocoa powder. Set aside.
3. Combine cocoa powder, water and milk in a saucepan and bring to a full boil, being careful not to boil over. Remove from heat and add oil. When mixture has cooled to lukewarm, stir in egg and vanilla.
4. Using an electric mixer, add dry ingredients to wet, beating just until smooth. Do not over-beat.
5. Line the bottom of a greased 8-inch round cake pan with a circular piece of wax paper. Pour in batter and bake for about 25-30 minutes. (Check centre for doneness with a skewer.) Cool in pan on a rack.
6. Remove cooled cake from pan and cut in half horizontally with a bread knife. Spread half the whipped cream on first layer. Place second layer on top. Spread raspberry sauce on top layer, then decorate edge with dollops of whipped cream. **SERVES 8**

Nutrients per serving: 422 calories, 8 g fat, 5 g protein, 64 g carbohydrates, 5 g fibre. Excellent source of fibre.

Chef's tip: Double or triple the recipe and keep extra cakes in the freezer for impromptu occasions. This super-moist cake also tastes great served with a simple dusting of icing sugar.

dutch chocolate cake

cooking 101
short-crust pastry

1. Sift all-purpose flour and salt into a large mixing bowl.

2. Drop in grated butter and cubed shortening, and lightly rub it into the flour with your fingertips until mixture has a coarse, mealy texture. Pour ice water around edges of mixture and press together to form a ball. The pastry will be marbled with flecks of butter and shortening.

3. Divide pastry in half. At this point, you may flatten each half into a 2-inch thick disc and wrap snugly in plastic wrap. Keeps up to one week in the fridge or three months in the freezer.

equipment

mixing bowls
measuring cups
paring knife
9-inch pie plate
sifter
grater
pastry brush
rolling pin

4. On a lightly floured surface, roll pastry out into two circles, 13 inches in diameter and $\frac{1}{4}$-inch thick. Line a 9-inch pie plate with one of the pastry rounds. Trim away excess.

ingredients

3	cups all-purpose flour
$\frac{1}{4}$	teaspoon salt
$\frac{1}{4}$	pound cold unsalted butter, coarsely grated
$\frac{1}{4}$	pound cold shortening, cut into half-inch cubes
$\frac{1}{4}$	cup ice water

5. Fill your pie with your favourite filling. (Try our Blue Ribbon Apple Pie, page 110.) Brush edge of pie shell with egg wash. Lay the top over filled shell and crimp edges to form a tight seal. Bake as directed.

blue ribbon apple pie

blue ribbon apple pie

snappy gingers

Blue Ribbon Apple Pie

	short-crust pastry (see page 108)
6-8	Royal Gala apples, peeled, cored and cut into ¼-inch slices
⅓	cup granulated sugar
¼	teaspoon cinnamon
¼	teaspoon ground nutmeg
½	teaspoon lemon zest
2	tablespoons unsalted butter, cold
	egg wash

1. Prepare pastry, line 9-inch pie plate and place pie top on a baking sheet. Refrigerate both.
2. Preheat oven to 425 F.
3. Toss apples with sugar, cinnamon, nutmeg and lemon zest. Spread apples into bottom of chilled pastry shell and dot butter in small pieces over apple filling.
4. Brush edge of pie shell with egg wash. Lay top over filled shell and crimp edges. Cut several small vents in top and brush with remaining egg wash.
5. Bake for 12 minutes at 425 F. Reduce heat to 350 F and continue baking for 1 hour. **MAKES ONE 9-INCH PIE**

Snappy Gingers

⅔	cup unsalted butter, room temperature
¼	cup dark-brown sugar, loosely packed
1	cup granulated sugar
1	egg yolk
2	tablespoons blackstrap molasses
1	cup all-purpose flour
½	teaspoon baking soda
1¼	teaspoons each ground ginger and ground cinnamon
½	teaspoon each ground cloves and ground allspice
1	tablespoon ground espresso
¼	teaspoon salt

1. Cream together butter, brown sugar and ½ cup granulated sugar until light and fluffy. Add egg yolk and molasses. Mix well. In a separate bowl, combine flour, baking soda, spices, espresso and salt. Mix these into butter mixture and refrigerate for 30 minutes.
2. Roll chilled dough into 2 logs, 1 inch in diameter. Wrap in waxed paper and freeze.
3. Preheat oven to 350 F. Remove dough from freezer, let stand for 10 minutes, unwrap and slice into ¼-inch rounds.
4. Dip top of each round in remaining sugar. Place rounds sugar-side up 2 inches apart on a parchment-lined baking sheet and bake for 10 to 12 minutes. **MAKES 3 DOZEN**

Nutrients per 2 cookies: 150 calories, 7 g fat, 1 g protein, 21 g carbohydrates.

sticky
toffee pudding

cooking 101: baking

- Baking is more scientific than savoury cooking, so measure carefully and be mindful of substitutions.

- Check the calibration of your oven. A couple of degrees can have a drastic impact on the results of your baked goods.

- Invest in good-quality bakeware and take care with cleaning and storage.

- The size of baking dishes and pans is essential. Check recipes for exact sizes.

- Practice makes perfect. Our grandmothers baked bread, pies and cookies regularly. Don't give up after the first try.

Sticky Toffee Pudding

1½   cups Irish whisky
1¼   cups dates, pitted and roughly chopped
2   teaspoons baking soda
2½   cups all-purpose flour
2   teaspoons baking powder
1   cup unsalted butter, room temperature
⅔   cup granulated sugar
4   eggs
2   teaspoons vanilla extract
    toffee sauce (see right)

1. Preheat oven to 350 F.
2. In a medium saucepan, combine whisky, dates and baking soda. Bring to a boil, remove from heat and cool.
3. Combine flour and baking powder together in a bowl.
4. With an electric mixer using a paddle attachment, cream butter and sugar together for 3-4 minutes until light and fluffy. Beat in eggs one at a time. Add vanilla and half of flour mixture. Mix in date mixture and remainder of flour mixture until well blended. Pour into a greased 12-cup Bundt pan and bake for 45 minutes.
5. Remove from oven and pour up to half of toffee sauce over cake and continue to bake for another 15 minutes or until a skewer inserted into cake comes out clean. Remove from oven and cool in pan for 10 minutes. Invert onto plate and serve with remaining toffee sauce. **SERVES 10**

Toffee Sauce

4   cups 35% cream
2   cups packed brown sugar
½   cup unsalted butter
½   cup Irish whisky

1. In a large, heavy-bottomed saucepan, combine all ingredients. Bring to a boil, stirring constantly. Reduce heat to a simmer.
2. Continue until sauce has reduced by half. **MAKES 3 CUPS**

Nutrients per serving: 1,237 calories, 67 g fat, 10 g protein, 126 g carbohydrates, 5 g fibre. High source of fibre. Excellent source of vitamins A and D, folic acid, thiamin, riboflavin and iron.

Caramel Sauce Two Ways

Creamy Caramel

1 ½   cups granulated sugar
½   cup water
1   cup 35% cream

1. In a large, heavy-bottomed saucepan, combine sugar and water. Place over high heat and stir to dissolve sugar. Use a pastry brush dipped in cold water to brush down crystallized sugar that forms on the sides of the pot.
2. Let mixture cook until a caramel colour begins to develop, about 5-7 minutes. Remove from heat and slowly whisk in cream, being watchful as it will sputter and bubble. Gently whisk until smooth and creamy. Ladle warm out of the pot, or cool caramel before storing. **MAKES 2 CUPS**

Nutrients per 2 tablespoons: 351 calories, 26 g fat, 1 g protein, 27 g carbohydrates. Excellent source of vitamin D.

Clear Caramel

2   tablespoons water
2   cups granulated sugar
2   cups apple juice
1   cinnamon stick
2   star anise

1. In a saucepan, combine water and sugar. Bring to a boil over high heat, and cook until syrup becomes amber, about 7 minutes. Remove from heat and slowly whisk in apple juice, being careful of the steam. Add cinnamon and star anise. Return to high heat and bring to a boil.
2. Lower heat and simmer until reduced to one cup of liquid, about 20 minutes. Discard cinnamon stick and star anise. **MAKES 1 CUP**

Nutrients per 2 tablespoons: 213 calories, 55 g carbohydrates.

Chef's tip: Store caramel sauces in plastic squeeze bottles in the fridge. Warm in the microwave for a minute just before serving. Try clear caramel on sponge cake or pancakes. The creamy sauce tastes great with ice cream, profiteroles or drizzled over berries with whipped cream.

creamy caramel

clear caramel

Macadamia Nut Brittle

1 ⅔   cups granulated sugar
½   cup water
¼   cup corn syrup
2 ½   tablespoons unsalted butter
¼   teaspoon baking soda
1 ½   cups macadamia nuts, toasted and roughly chopped
¼   teaspoon salt

1. Line a baking sheet with parchment paper. Spray an off-set spatula with non-stick spray.
2. In a heavy-bottomed saucepan over medium-high heat, combine sugar, water, corn syrup and butter. Stir to dissolve sugar and cook until a golden caramel colour has developed, about 10 minutes.
3. Remove caramel from heat and stir in baking soda, nuts and salt. Working quickly using an off-set spatula, spread mixture as thinly as possible onto baking sheet. Caution should be used when working with this hot mixture.
4. Let cool completely and break brittle into pieces. Store in an airtight container. **SERVES 10**

Nutrients per serving: 264 calories, 15 g fat, 1 g protein, 35 g carbohydrates, 2 g fibre.

macadamia nut brittle

crockpot chocolate cake

blackberry gratin

Crockpot Chocolate Cake

1	package chocolate-cake mix
1	cup sour cream
1	cup water
4	eggs
¾	cup vegetable oil
1	package instant chocolate-pudding mix
1	cup chopped bittersweet chocolate

1. Spray slow cooker with non-stick spray. Mix all ingredients in a bowl, pour into slow cooker and cover.
2. For a slow cooker with a 6-quart capacity, cook on high for 2 hours. Cake is done when an inserted wooden skewer comes out clean.
3. Scoop servings out of pot with a spoon. Serve warm with vanilla ice cream. **SERVES 8**

Nutrients per serving: 690 calories, 46 g fat, 10 g protein, 71 g carbohydrates, 2 g fibre. Excellent source of vitamins D and E, folic acid, iron and phosphorus.

Blackberry Gratin

4	egg yolks
6	tablespoons granulated sugar
½	cup Sauternes or icewine
⅔	cup 35% cream, whipped to a soft peak
3	pints blackberries
	icing sugar for dusting

1. Place egg yolks, sugar and wine in a large stainless-steel bowl. Place bowl over a pot of simmering water, making sure bowl does not touch the water. Heat mixture, whisking constantly. It will begin to thicken and double in volume. Remove from heat, and continue whisking until completely cool. This mixture is called sabayon – or zabaglione. Fold whipped cream into sabayon.
2. Move oven rack to top position and preheat broiler.
3. Divide blackberries into 6 individual gratin dishes. Spoon sabayon over berries and sprinkle generously with icing sugar. Place under broiler and brown for approximately 2 minutes. Remove from oven, dust with more icing sugar and serve. **SERVES 6**

Nutrients per serving: 216 calories, 6 g fat, 3 g protein, 35 g carbohydrates, 8 g fibre. Excellent source of vitamins C and D, and folic acid.

extreme
chocolate cookies

scottish tablet

Extreme Chocolate Cookies

1	cup granulated sugar
4	eggs
1	teaspoon vanilla extract
1/2	teaspoon salt
1/2	cup all-purpose flour
1/4	tablespoon baking powder
1	pound bittersweet chocolate, melted
1	pound white chocolate, chopped into 1/4-inch pieces

1. Preheat the oven to 325 F.
2. Whisk together sugar, eggs, vanilla extract and salt in a large mixing bowl until pale yellow in colour. Add melted dark chocolate.
3. In a separate bowl, mix together flour and baking powder. Add dry ingredients to egg and chocolate mixture, and stir in white chocolate pieces.
4. Working quickly, drop generous tablespoon-sized portions of batter 2 inches apart onto a parchment-lined baking sheet. Bake for 10 to 12 minutes and don't be tempted to over-bake. Transfer to a wire rack to cool completely. **MAKES 3 DOZEN**

Nutrients per 2 cookies: 329 calories, 19 g fat, 5 g protein, 41 g carbohydrates.

Scottish Tablet

1/2	cup unsalted butter
3/4	cup homogenized milk
1/2	375 ml-can sweetened condensed milk
5	cups granulated sugar
1	teaspoon vanilla extract

1. In a large saucepan, melt butter over medium-high heat. Add both milks and stir to combine. Add sugar and stir. Bring mixture to a boil until a candy thermometer reads 240 F. This will take approximately 12 minutes.
Caution: This mixture is extremely hot.
2. Remove from heat. Quickly add vanilla and beat with an electric mixer for about 2 minutes until you feel the texture has become grainy. The mixture should still have a pourable consistency. Pour into a non-stick 8" x 8" pan. Let cool, remove from pan and cut into bars. **SERVES 12**

Nutrients per serving: 423 calories, 10 g fat, 2 g protein, 85 g carbohydrates.

oatmeal cranberry flaxseed cookies

Oatmeal Cranberry Flaxseed Cookies

½   cup canola oil
¼   cup brown sugar
½   cup granulated sugar
1   egg
1   teaspoon vanilla extract
½   cup all-purpose flour
½   cup flaxseed, ground
½   teaspoon baking soda
½   cup dried cranberries
1   cup rolled oats

1. Preheat oven to 350 F.
2. In a bowl, mix canola oil and sugars together.
Add egg and vanilla, mixing well. Add flour, ground
flaxseed and baking soda, and mix until well combined.
Stir in cranberries and rolled oats.
3. Drop generous-sized tablespoons of dough, 2 inches
apart, on a parchment-lined baking sheet. Bake for 10-12
minutes. **MAKES 2 DOZEN**

*Nutrients per cookie: 86 calories, 1 g protein, 4 g fat,
10 g carbohydrates, 1 g fibre, 0.5 g omega-3.*

Crème Caramel

1¼   cups granulated sugar
⅓   cup water
4   egg yolks
1   cup milk
1   cup 35% cream
1½   teaspoons vanilla extract

1. Preheat oven to 325 F.
2. Place ⅔ cup sugar and water in a heavy-bottomed
saucepan over low heat. Let sugar dissolve. Using a pastry
brush, carefully brush walls of pot with a little water to
prevent sugar from crystallizing on the sides. Increase heat
to medium-high and boil until syrup turns golden. Remove
from heat promptly and carefully divide hot caramel
among six 4-ounce ramekins and set aside.
3. Whisk together egg yolks, remaining sugar and vanilla
in a large mixing bowl. Set aside.
4. In a medium saucepan, bring milk and cream just to a
boil. Turn heat off. Gently whisk 2 tablespoons of hot milk
mixture into egg mixture. To prevent excessive bubbles,
slowly whisk in remaining hot milk mixture ⅓ at a time.
Strain through a fine sieve.
5. Line a baking dish with a paper towel. Place ramekins
evenly spaced in bottom of dish. Pour ½ cup custard
mixture into ramekins. Put into oven on the outside edge
of middle rack. Carefully pour boiling water into baking
dish until it's ⅔ of the way up ramekins (be careful not to
get any water on the custard mixture). Cover baking dish
with aluminum foil and very gently slide dish to centre of
rack for even baking.
6. Bake for about 35 minutes or until custards are almost
set – they should have a slight jiggle when they come out.
Remove dish from oven, and use tongs to remove custards
from water bath. Let stand at room temperature for 5
minutes, then refrigerate until well chilled.
7. To serve, dip ramekin in very hot water for 15 to 20
seconds. Run a sharp knife around sides of ramekin.
Invert custard onto plate. The caramel will pool around it.
SERVES 6

*Nutrients per serving: 354 calories, 18 g fat, 4 g protein,
45 g carbohydrates. Excellent source of vitamins B_{12} and D.
Good source of vitamin A.*

crème caramel

20-minute *suppers*

chef's tip Drizzle olive oil on top of pesto to help keep its vibrant colour. Double the pesto recipe and store extra in the fridge or freeze in small batches.

shopping list

- ☐ garlic
- ☐ pine nuts
- ☐ parmesan
- ☐ fresh basil
- ☐ extra-virgin olive oil
- ☐ pasta
- ☐ whole chicken, pre-roasted
- ☐ cherry tomatoes

Pesto Chicken Pasta

1. In a food processor, chop 3 cloves **garlic**. Add ½ cup toasted **pine nuts**, 1 cup grated **Parmesan**, 3 cups washed, loosely packed **fresh basil leaves** and ½ teaspoon **salt**. With the motor running, slowly pour in ⅔ cup **extra-virgin olive oil** until well blended.

2. In a large pot of salted, boiling water, cook 1 box (500 g) **pasta** until al dente. Meanwhile, pull **chicken** meat off the bone and cut into bite-sized pieces.

3. Drain pasta, and while still hot, toss with pesto and 1 pint halved **cherry tomatoes.** Add chicken and garnish with shaved Parmesan.
SERVES 6

Nutrients per serving: 890 calories, 51 g fat, 47 g protein, 61 g carbohydrates, 5 g fibre. High source of fibre. Excellent source of vitamins B_6, B_{12} and E, folate, niacin, thiamin, riboflavin, pantothenic acid, calcium, iron, zinc, phosphorus and magnesium.

Wine Pairing
The pear and citrus flavours of Pinot Grigio are an excellent match for pesto pastas.

pesto chicken pasta

nutrition Omega-3s are not manufactured by the body and the only way to get them is through your diet. Four ounces of salmon contains 2 grams of omega-3 fatty acids.

shopping list

- ☐ salmon filets
- ☐ lemon olive oil
- ☐ fresh tarragon
- ☐ fresh marjoram
- ☐ fresh thyme
- ☐ fresh chives
- ☐ lemon
- ☐ asparagus
- ☐ acini di pepe pasta
- ☐ cherry tomatoes

Lemon Baked Salmon

1. Preheat oven to 375 F.

2. Bring a large pot of well-salted water to a boil.

3. Place six 5-ounce **salmon filets** on a parchment-lined baking sheet. Drizzle each filet with ½ teaspoon **lemon olive oil**. Season with **salt** and **pepper**.

4. Mix together 2 tablespoons each of chopped **tarragon, marjoram, thyme** and **grated lemon zest**. Divide and sprinkle the herb mixture over the filets.

5. In the boiling water, blanch 12 **asparagus spears** for 2 minutes. Save the blanching water to cook your pasta. Cut asparagus into 1-inch pieces.

6. Cook 1 box (500 g) **acini di pepe pasta** until al dente, approximately 8 minutes. While pasta is cooking, place salmon into oven and cook for 8-10 minutes. Drain pasta and mix with ½ pint halved **cherry tomatoes**, asparagus pieces, 1 tablespoon **lemon juice**, ¼ cup **chopped chives** and 1 teaspoon **salt**. Serve salmon on a bed of the pasta mixture.
SERVES 6

Nutrients per serving: 635 calories, 20 g fat, 43 g protein, 70 g carbohydrates, 5 g fibre. Excellent source of vitamins B_6, B_{12} and good source of vitamins C and E.

Wine Pairing
The dry, crisp acidity and fruit finish of unoaked Chardonnay matches well with both fish and herbs.

lemon baked salmon

quick side Place 1 cup of instant couscous in a bowl and drizzle with lemon olive oil. Add just enough boiling water to cover. Seal with plastic wrap and let stand for 5 minutes. Serve.

shopping list

- ☐ vegetable oil
- ☐ chicken breasts
- ☐ shallots
- ☐ garlic
- ☐ chicken stock
- ☐ white wine
- ☐ canned plum tomatoes
- ☐ black olives, pitted
- ☐ capers
- ☐ fresh parsley
- ☐ fresh basil

Chicken Provençal

1. Heat 1 tablespoon **vegetable oil** in a large sauté pan over medium-high heat. Add four 6-ounce skinless, boneless **chicken breasts** and sear on both sides until well browned. Remove chicken from pan and set aside.

2. Reduce heat and add another tablespoon of oil to pan. Add 2 finely chopped **shallots**, 3 minced cloves **garlic** and sauté for 2 minutes. Add ½ cup **chicken stock**, ¼ cup **white wine**, one can (14 oz.) chopped **plum tomatoes** and simmer until mixture thickens slightly. Return chicken to pan and simmer until cooked through, about 5 minutes.

3. Remove chicken from skillet and set aside on platter. Stir ½ cup pitted chopped **black olives**, 2 tablespoons **capers** and ¼ cup **parsley** into sauce. Spoon sauce over chicken and garnish with ¼ cup chopped **basil**. **SERVES 4**

Nutrients per serving: 339 calories, 13 g fat, 43 g protein, 11 g carbohydrates, 5 g fibre. High source of fibre. Excellent source of vitamins B_6 and E, folate and magnesium. Good source of vitamin C.

Wine Pairing
An oaky Chardonnay works just fine, but try venturing into the earthiness of Pinot Noir.

chicken provençal

toppings
zucchini, red onion, feta cheese & fresh thyme ◆ smoked chicken, pesto, cherry tomatoes & fontina ◆ sausage, cooked potato, grated Parmesan & truffle oil ◆ grilled shrimp, spinach, goat cheese & lemon olive oil ◆ smoked salmon, ricotta, green onions & lemon zest

shopping list

☐ pitas

☐ black olive pesto

☐ arugula

☐ smoked provolone

☐ roasted red peppers

☐ marinated artichokes

Mediterranean Pita Pizzas

1. Preheat oven to 400 F.

2. Place 7-inch **pitas** on a baking sheet and top with **black olive pesto, arugula, smoked provolone, roasted red peppers** and **marinated artichokes.** Load it up any way you like.

3. Fire into the oven for 10-12 minutes or until cheese melts. **1 PER PERSON**

Nutrients per pizza: 487 calories, 23 g protein, 25 g fat, 43 g carbohydrates, 5 g fibre. Excellent source of vitamins A, B_{12} and C. Good source of iron and dietary fibre.

Wine Pairing
Sangiovese, a light-bodied red wine with a fresh and fruity bouquet, is a great companion to pizza and other Italian food.

mediterranean pita pizzas

127

chef's tip If you can't make it to your local Asian grocery store (or shimmy up a banana tree), substitute parchment paper for banana leaves to get the same great flavour results.

shopping list

- ☐ halibut filets
- ☐ banana leaves
- ☐ lemon olive oil
- ☐ thai chilies
- ☐ oranges
- ☐ lemon
- ☐ ginger
- ☐ green onions
- ☐ star anise
- ☐ butcher's twine

Halibut En Papillote

1. Preheat oven to 450 F.

2. Lay out 4 **banana leaves** (15" x 10") and brush each with 1 tablespoon **lemon olive oil**.

3. Mix together 4 roughly chopped **Thai chilies**, zest of 2 **oranges** and 1 **lemon**, a 3-inch piece **fresh ginger**, peeled and julienned, 4 **green onions**, thinly sliced. Place 1 tablespoon of the mixture in middle of each banana leaf. Place four 5-ounce **halibut filets** (skin removed) on top of chili mixture and season with salt and pepper. Top fish with remaining chili mixture and one piece **star anise**.

4. Combine the **citrus juices** from the oranges and lemon, and drizzle 3 tablespoons over each filet. Gather opposite corners of banana leaf to meet and tie with **butcher's twine**. Place on a baking sheet and bake for 15 minutes. Remove from oven and let rest 5 minutes before serving.
SERVES 4

Nutrients per serving: 316 calories, 17 g fat, 30 g protein, 10 g carbohydrates, 1 g fibre. Excellent source of vitamins B_6, B_{12}, C, D and E, niacin, phosphorus and magnesium. Good source of folate.

Wine Pairing
A dry Riesling is the perfect companion to this dish. The subtle sweetness of the wine enhances the aromatics and tempers the chilies.

halibut en papillote

market When purchasing mussels, look for shiny black, uncracked shells that are tightly closed. After cooking, discard any cracked or unopened shells. Mussels are best in months that have an "r" in their names.

shopping list

- ☐ unsalted butter
- ☐ fresh thyme
- ☐ shallots
- ☐ garlic
- ☐ celery
- ☐ leeks
- ☐ white wine
- ☐ crème fraîche
- ☐ mussels
- ☐ fresh parsley
- ☐ french bread

Drink Pairing
Unoaked and medium-dry white wines are the best choice for cooking and accompanying mussels. ◆ Medium- to full-bodied beers are also favourite matches, both in the pot and on the table.

Moules Marinière

1. Melt ¼ cup **unsalted butter** in a large pot with 4 sprigs **thyme**.

2. Thinly slice 5 **shallots**, 4 cloves **garlic**, 2 stalks **celery**, 2 **leeks** and add to pot. Sauté until softened but not browned, about 15 minutes. Add 1 cup **white wine**, 2 teaspoons cracked **black pepper**, ½ teaspoon **salt** and ¼ cup **crème fraîche**. Increase heat to high and bring to a boil. Add 2 pounds **P.E.I. mussels** and gently stir. Cover with a tightly fitting lid and cook for approximately 3-5 minutes, or until mussels have opened. Turn heat off, add ¼ cup chopped **parsley** and gently stir.

3. Serve in large bowls with French bread. **SERVES 2**

Nutrients per serving: 173 calories, 5 g protein, 9 g fat, 6 g carbohydrates, 2 g fibre. Excellent source of vitamin B_{12} and iron.

moules marinière

chef's tip Soak wooden skewers in water at least an hour prior to cooking to keep them from burning. Metal skewers offer more stability for firmer cuts of meat and vegetables. They also cook foods faster, because the metal heats up. Double skewer delicate foods (like scallops) to make turning easier.

shopping list

- ☐ english cucumbers
- ☐ black olives
- ☐ red pepper
- ☐ mini bocconcini
- ☐ red-wine vinegar
- ☐ extra-virgin olive oil
- ☐ pre-marinated kebabs

Grilled Kebabs & Cucumber Ribbon Salad

1. Cut two **English cucumbers** in half widthwise and peel into ribbons with a vegetable peeler.

2. Toss cucumber ribbons with ½ cup pitted **black olives**, ½ cup finely chopped **red pepper**, 1 cup **mini bocconcini**, 2 tablespoons **red-wine vinegar** and ¼ cup **extra-virgin olive oil**. Season with **salt** and **pepper**.

3. Grill 1-2 pre-marinated **kebabs** (your choice of chicken, pork, beef, shrimp, vegetarian, etc.) per person for approximately 15 minutes over a medium-high heat or until cooked through, turning occasionally.
SERVES 4

Nutrients per serving (2 kebabs + salad): 443 calories, 19 g fat, 58 g protein, 8 g carbohydrates, 2 g fibre. Excellent source of vitamins A, C and E, calcium and phosphorus.

Wine Pairing
The herbaceous nose of Sauvignon Blanc pairs nicely with the flavours of the grill. A great wine for summer – try it as an apéritif. Goes well with seafood, too.

grilled kebabs (chicken) &
cucumber ribbon salad

leftovers When making osso bucco, remove meat from any leftover pieces and add them back to the remaining tomato sauce and you've got a hearty ragout to serve with penne or rigatoni.

shopping list

- ☐ olive oil
- ☐ carrots
- ☐ onion
- ☐ celery
- ☐ veal shank
- ☐ garlic
- ☐ fresh sage leaves
- ☐ white wine
- ☐ tomato paste
- ☐ instant polenta or white cannelli beans
- ☐ crushed tomatoes
- ☐ parsley

Osso Bucco

1. Pour ¼ cup **olive oil** into the bottom of a slow cooker.

2. Add 3 roughly chopped **carrots**, 1 roughly chopped medium **onion**, and 3 roughly chopped stalks **celery**. Place 6 pieces **veal shank** over the vegetables.

3. Scatter 20 crushed cloves **garlic**, ½ bunch chopped Italian **parsley** and 8 **sage** leaves around the veal. Pour in ½ cup **white wine**, one 28-ounce can **crushed tomatoes** and 2 tablespoons **tomato paste**. Season generously with **salt** and **pepper**, set pot to low heat and cook for 6 hours.

4. Just before serving, cook 1 cup instant **polenta** to serve with veal shanks – or add 1 can drained **white cannelli beans** to slow cooker to round out the meal. **SERVES 6**

Nutrients per serving: 331 calories, 31 g protein, 13 g fat, 25 g carbohydrates, 5 g fibre. A good source of vitamin C.

Wine Pairing
For rich, slow-cooked stews, serve red wines with big hearts like Amarones or Cabernet Sauvignons.

osso bucco

135

pantry
extras

sauces • dressings • marinades • vinaigrettes

rubs • sides • oils • stocks • soups

Aioli

1   egg
1   teaspoon Dijon mustard
2   tablespoons lemon juice
2   cloves garlic, minced
1½   cups vegetable oil
½   teaspoon salt

1. Place egg, Dijon mustard, lemon juice and garlic in a food processor. **2.** Turn machine on and very slowly pour in half the vegetable oil and add salt. **3.** Pour in remaining vegetable oil drip by drip until mixture emulsifies.

Béarnaise Sauce

½   cup white wine
½   cup unsalted butter
4   egg yolks
2   tablespoons finely chopped shallots
2   tablespoons chopped fresh tarragon
½   teaspoon salt
2   teaspoons lemon juice

1. Place white wine in a non-reactive pot. **2.** Boil for 5 minutes until the wine is reduced by half. **3.** Melt butter over high heat in a small pot, and skim the foam from the top as it rises. **4.** Place egg yolks into a bowl and whisk in reduced wine. **5.** Drizzle hot butter into egg yolks while whisking constantly. **6.** Bring a pot of water to a boil and remove from the heat. **7.** Place the bowl with egg mixture over the pot and whisk until the mixture has thickened enough to coat the back of a spoon, about 1 minute. **8.** Stir in shallots, salt and lemon juice. **9.** Fold in chopped tarragon. **SERVES 4**

Cranberry Vinaigrette

¼   cup fresh orange juice
¼   cup pure cranberry juice
1   tablespoon Dijon mustard
2   tablespoons cider vinegar
½   teaspoon salt
½   cup vegetable oil
¼   cup olive oil

1. Combine all ingredients except oils in a mixing bowl. **2.** With a whisk, mix in the oils, one at a time, in a slow, steady stream. Store in refrigerator for up to 2 weeks, but give it a quick whisk before you dress your greens.
MAKES 1½ CUPS

Chermoula Marinade

1   pinch saffron
2   tablespoons fresh lemon juice
2   teaspoons cumin seeds, toasted
2   teaspoons coriander seeds, toasted
¼   cup pine nuts, toasted
2   red Thai chilies, roughly chopped
2   cloves garlic, roughly chopped
1   lemon, zested
1   bunch cilantro, stems and leaves
1   bunch mint, leaves only
½   cup olive oil

1. Soak saffron in lemon juice for 5 minutes. **2.** Place cumin seeds, coriander seeds, pine nuts, chilies, lemon zest, garlic and saffron/lemon juice mixture in a food processor and pulse until combined. With processor running, add cilantro, mint leaves and slowly pour in olive oil.

Chive Oil

1   bunch fresh chives, chopped
1   cup vegetable oil
1   clove garlic, finely minced
1   pinch salt

1. Place all ingredients in a food processor or blender.
2. Purée until smooth. Place in a squeeze bottle and refrigerate. **MAKES 1 CUP**

Warm Cider Dressing

Intensely flavourful no-fat dressing option – also great as a sauté sauce.

⅓   cup maple syrup
⅓   cup cider vinegar
3   tablespoons cognac or brandy
1   tablespoon mustard seeds

Combine all ingredients and mix well. Reduce slightly to light syrup. **MAKES ¾ CUP**

Classic Crepes

6   eggs
1   cup milk
1   cup all-purpose flour
1   pinch salt

1. Using an electric mixer, beat eggs, milk, flour and salt, resulting in a thin batter that should coat the back of a spoon.
2. Heat a 6-inch non-stick pan over medium heat and add 2 tablespoons of batter into the pan. Allow batter to cover the entire surface of pan. When tiny holes appear on the surface of the batter, flip crepe and finish cooking. Do not let crepe brown. Remove from pan, transfer to a plate and continue cooking crepes, stacking each one with parchment paper in between. **MAKES 18 CREPES**

Dashi Stock

1   piece kombu, 6" x 3"
8   cups cold water
3   cups bonito flakes

1. Place kombu in a large pot with 3 cups cold water. Simmer until kombu is tender. Remove kombu and add bonito flakes with remaining water. Simmer for 3 minutes. **2.** Remove pot from heat and allow bonito flakes to infuse for 30 minutes. Strain through a fine mesh strainer.
MAKES 8 CUPS

Dijon Vinaigrette

1   tablespoon Dijon mustard
3   tablespoons red-wine vinegar
½   teaspoon salt
½   cup grapeseed oil

1. Whisk together mustard, vinegar and salt. **2.** Pour in grapeseed oil in a slow steady stream, whisking constantly until thickened. Set aside. **MAKES ¾ CUP**

Ginger Marinade

A versatile sauce – wonderful with fish, pork and chicken.

2   tablespoons grated fresh ginger
1   clove garlic, minced
1   tablespoon honey
3   tablespoons fish sauce
3   tablespoons lime juice
2   tablespoons water
1   teaspoon Tabasco

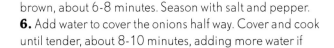

Combine all ingredients in a bowl. Marinate meats for 30 minutes or in refrigerator overnight. **MAKES ⅔ CUP**

Glazed Pearl Onions

1   10-ounce bag white pearl onions
1   tablespoon unsalted butter
1   tablespoon olive oil
2   sprigs fresh thyme
1   teaspoon finely chopped fresh rosemary
1   bay leaf
1   teaspoon salt
½   teaspoon cracked black pepper
1   tablespoon dried currants
1   tablespoon honey
1   tablespoon sherry vinegar

1. To remove the skins of the pearl onions, blanch for 1 minute in a pot of boiling water. **2.** Using a paring knife, peel away the skin and discard. **3.** Melt butter and oil in a skillet over medium-high heat. **4.** Add thyme, rosemary, bay leaf and peeled onions. **5.** Sauté until onions begin to brown, about 6-8 minutes. Season with salt and pepper. **6.** Add water to cover the onions half way. Cover and cook until tender, about 8-10 minutes, adding more water if needed. **7.** Increase heat to high and add currants, honey and vinegar. **8.** Stirring constantly, cook until syrupy and onions are glazed, about 5 minutes. **9.** Discard the bay leaf and thyme, and add seasoning if necessary.

Laksa Paste

1   tablespoon chopped fresh ginger
1   clove garlic, roughly chopped
¼   cup roughly chopped shallots
1   tablespoon red curry paste
½   cup coconut milk
1   tablespoon vegetable oil

Put all ingredients in a blender and process until smooth. Store in refrigerator or freeze. **MAKES 1 CUP**

Masala Orange Zest Rub

Try this flavour booster with white fish, shrimp or pork.

2   tablespoons garam masala
1   tablespoon sesame seeds
1   teaspoon garlic powder
1   teaspoon ground ginger
½   teaspoon salt
1   tablespoon orange zest
2   tablespoons fresh orange juice
1   tablespoon olive oil

Combine all ingredients to form a paste.

Mini Veal Meatballs

1   pound ground veal
1   egg
½   cup finely grated Parmesan
1   clove garlic, minced
¼   cup fresh Italian parsley, chopped
2   tablespoons olive oil
    salt and pepper to taste

1. Combine all ingredients, except olive oil, until well mixed. **2.** Roll mixture into meatballs the size of a quarter and place on a parchment-lined tray in a single layer. Refrigerate meatballs for 2 hours before cooking. **3.** Fry meatballs in olive oil until golden brown. Set aside on paper towels.
MAKES 3 DOZEN

Mint Sauce

1	cup red-wine vinegar
1/4	cup brown sugar
2	cups fresh mint leaves
1	cup fresh Italian parsley leaves
1	shallot, roughly chopped
1	clove garlic
1	cup olive oil
1/2	teaspoon salt

1. Combine red-wine vinegar and brown sugar in a small pot and bring to a boil, stirring to dissolve the sugar. **2.** Simmer until the liquid has reduced to a syrupy consistency, approximately 5 minutes. Let cool. **3.** Purée the mint, parsley, shallot, garlic and salt in a food processor. **4.** With the processor running, pour in the cooled sugar mixture and olive oil. **MAKES 1 1/2 CUPS**

Mushroom Stock

1/4	cup mixed dried mushrooms
1	cup boiling water
1/4	cup olive oil
2	onions, sliced
1/2	bunch fresh thyme
3	cloves garlic, crushed
6	cups sliced button mushrooms
4	cups shiitake mushroom stems
1	cup white wine
14	cups cold water

1. Soak dried mushrooms in boiling water. **2.** Heat olive oil over high heat in a large stock pot and add onions and thyme, cooking until golden. **3.** Add garlic and mushrooms and continue to cook for 5 more minutes over a medium heat. **4.** Deglaze with wine to lift any bits off the bottom of the pan. **5.** Add cold water, rehydrated mushrooms and their liquid to the pot. Simmer for 30 minutes and strain through a fine sieve. **6.** Cool and refrigerate. Stock can be divided into small amounts and frozen for up to three months. **MAKES 14 CUPS**

Parmesan Tuiles

1/4	cup coarsely grated Parmesan
1/4	cup coarsely grated Gruyère

1. Preheat oven to 375 F. **2.** Mix Parmesan and Gruyère together. Place a 2 1/2-inch round cookie cutter on a baking sheet lined with parchment paper. Sprinkle 1 tablespoon of cheese mixture into cutter. Lift cutter and repeat with remaining mixture. **3.** Bake for 6-7 minutes or until lightly golden. Allow to fully cool on parchment paper. **MAKES 6 TO 8**

Raspberry Sauce

2 1/2	cups frozen raspberries, in syrup
1/4	cup cornstarch

Bring frozen raspberries with cornstarch to a rolling boil, then cool. Use warm for sauce or cold as filling for pie or cake.

Red Onion Marmalade

1/3	cup olive oil
4	large red onions, thinly sliced
1	tablespoon salt
3/4	cup granulated sugar
3/4	cup ruby port
3/4	cup red-wine vinegar
1	tablespoon chopped fresh thyme

1. Warm olive oil and red onions in a large saucepan over medium heat. **2.** Cook for 7 minutes or until very soft, stirring frequently. **3.** Add salt and sugar, and cook for a further 8 minutes. **4.** Add port, red-wine vinegar and thyme, and bring to a boil. **5.** Reduce heat to a simmer and continue cooking for another 20 minutes. **6.** Cool slightly. **Chef's tip:** Make red onion marmalade ahead of time and store in an airtight container. It's great on grilled meats or as an addition to your cheese tray.

Remoulade

A traditional French mayonnaise-based sauce, an excellent match with fish.

1	egg yolk
1/2	teaspoon salt
2	tablespoons lemon juice
2	tablespoons grainy mustard
3/4	cup grapeseed oil
1/4	cup capers, rinsed & chopped
1	tablespoon finely chopped shallots
3	tablespoons chopped gherkins
1	tablespoon chopped fresh Italian parsley
1	tablespoon chopped fresh chives
1	tablespoon finely chopped fresh tarragon
1	tablespoon fresh chervil leaves

1. Combine egg yolk, salt, lemon juice and grainy mustard together in a food processor. **2.** With processor running, very slowly pour grapeseed oil in a thin, steady stream. Transfer to a medium bowl. **3.** Add remaining ingredients. **4.** Stir to combine. Refrigerate until needed.

Roasted Red Pepper Soup

3	tablespoons vegetable oil
1	cup thinly sliced white onion
2	cloves garlic, minced
1	28-ounce can crushed tomatoes
5	red peppers, roasted and coarsely chopped
2	teaspoons canned chipotle peppers, chopped

5   cups chicken stock
1   orange, zested
1   teaspoon sugar
3   teaspoons kosher salt

1. In a stainless-steel pot, heat vegetable oil over medium-high heat. **2.** Add onion and garlic, and sauté until soft. **3.** Add remaining ingredients except orange zest, sugar and salt. Simmer for 25 minutes. Remove from heat and cool 10-15 minutes. **4.** In a food processor, purée mixture in small batches. **5.** Finish by adding orange zest, sugar and salt. **SERVES 6**

Smoky Citrus Rub

Add a little zing to chicken, salmon or lamb.

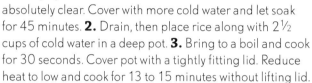

2   tablespoons smoked paprika
1   tablespoon dried mint
½   teaspoon salt
½   teaspoon pepper
2   tablespoons lemon zest
1   tablespoon minced garlic
2   tablespoons olive oil

Combine all ingredients to form a paste.

Spicy Mayonnaise

2   cloves garlic, minced
2   egg yolks
1   tablespoon Dijon mustard
2   tablespoons fresh lemon juice
1   teaspoon salt
1   teaspoon sambal oelek or your favourite hot sauce
1   cup vegetable oil

1. In a food processor or blender, combine garlic, yolks, mustard, lemon juice, salt and sambal olek. **2.** While the machine is running, slowly add the vegetable oil to emulsify. Add more hot sauce for desired spiciness. Refrigerate for up to one week.
Chef's tip: Add up to 1 tablespoon of your favourite hot sauce to cup of store-bought mayonnaise.

Sundried Tomato Vinaigrette

2   whole sundried tomatoes, packed in oil
1   clove garlic
½   cup olive oil
¼   cup red-wine vinegar
1   teaspoon balsamic vinegar
¼   teaspoon salt
¼   teaspoon cracked black pepper
¼   cup extra-virgin olive oil
1   teaspoon fresh oregano leaves

1. Purée sundried tomatoes and garlic in a food processor. **2.** Add olive oil, vinegars, salt and pepper. **3.** With food processor running, slowly pour in extra-virgin olive oil. **4.** Add oregano and pulse to combine. **MAKES 1 CUP**

Sushi Rice

2½   cups short-grained white sushi rice
2½   cups cold water
¼   cup rice vinegar
3   tablespoons granulated sugar
2   tablespoons mirin (sweet rice wine)
3   teaspoons salt

1. Place rice in a large bowl and cover with cold water. Stir with hands, but avoid grinding. Strain and rinse thoroughly until water becomes absolutely clear. Cover with more cold water and let soak for 45 minutes. **2.** Drain, then place rice along with 2½ cups of cold water in a deep pot. **3.** Bring to a boil and cook for 30 seconds. Cover pot with a tightly fitting lid. Reduce heat to low and cook for 13 to 15 minutes without lifting lid. **4.** Remove pot from heat and leave covered to steam for 10 minutes. **5.** Meanwhile, mix rice vinegar, sugar, mirin and salt, stirring until sugar and salt are completely dissolved. Spread cooked rice out into a large dish or baking sheet. **6.** Pour mixture over rice and mix thoroughly with your hands or a rice paddle. **7.** Fan rice until it has cooled to room temperature. Once cooled, the rice will separate easily and have a glossy sheen. **MAKES 6 CUPS**

Thai Dressing

½   cup water
½   cup granulated sugar
½   cup soy sauce
¼   cup rice vinegar
3   tablespoons sesame oil
2   cloves garlic, minced
3   tablespoons minced fresh ginger
1   teaspoon red chili flakes
2   tablespoons mirin

1. Combine sugar and water in a pot and cook until the sugar has just dissolved. **2.** Mix remaining ingredients with sugar syrup.

Watercress Mustard Oil

½   tablespoon mustard seeds
2   lemons, juiced
½   bunch watercress
1   teaspoon salt
1   cup grapeseed oil

1. Place mustard seeds in a sauté pan and toast over medium heat until seeds begin to pop. **2.** Put into blender with lemon juice, ½ bunch of watercress and salt. With motor running, slowly add grapeseed oil until well blended.

a-z
culinary guide

A

ACINI DI PEPE
Tiny pearls of pasta that lend themselves well to making all kinds of salads. A little goes a long way.

AIOLI [eye-OH-lee]
A traditional garlic mayonnaise that originated in the south of France.

ANTIOXIDANTS
Free-radical fighting compounds found in plant foods. They help prevent the buildup of fatty deposits in the bloodstream that can lead to stroke or heart disease. Different colours in fruits and veggies indicate the presence of antioxidants and other nutrients. Eating a full spectrum of coloured food is a good way to cover the bases and bolster your defence against disease. Many nutritional experts advise eating more than five plant foods a day, choosing vegetables and fruits in deep colours such as dark green, yellow, orange and red. See chart below.

B

BERRY (buying, storing, freezing)
Unlike other fruits, berries don't ripen further after picking, so only buy those that are ripe. Inspect fruit by looking at the bottom of the container to make sure it is not squashed or mouldy. Berries should be consumed within a day or two of buying. Keep them in the fridge in their packaging or on a paper towel-lined plate with some plastic wrap over top. Because berries freeze well, you can savour their fresh flavour all year long. **To freeze:** Spread berries in a single layer on parchment-lined baking sheets and freeze until solid. Scoop into plastic bags, label and return to freezer. **To defrost:** Transfer to the fridge so they thaw slowly or use directly from the freezer in smoothies or pancakes.

BLANCH
A method of cooking vegetables to maintain vibrant colour and texture, and retain nutrients. **How to:** Drop vegetables into boiling, well-salted water. Cook until tender but still al dente, 1-4 minutes, depending on the vegetable. Remove and plunge ▸

		Food Sources	Benefits
Red		Cooked tomatoes,* pink grapefruit,* guava, beets, kidney beans, red apples,* raspberries, red cabbage,* watermelon* and red peppers.*	Contain **lycopene** and **anthocyanins**, which help reduce lung and prostate cancer risk, lower blood pressure and maintain urinary-tract health.
Orange		Apricots, butternut squash, cantaloupes, carrots,* mangoes, peaches, pumpkins* and sweet potatoes.*	Contain **beta carotene**, which reduces risk of certain cancers and heart disease, helps maintain good vision and increases infection-fighting capability.
Yellow		Apricots, clementines, grapefruit, lemons,* nectarines and oranges.*	Contain **bioflavonoids**, which work with vitamin C to reduce the risk of some cancers and disease.
Green		Broccoli,* peas, honeydew melon, kale, kiwi,* leafy greens,* arugula, Brussels sprouts,* cabbage* and Swiss chard.	Contain **lutein** and **zeaxanthin**. Help maintain good vision and protect against macular degeneration (a physical disturbance in the retina that can cause blindness), cataracts and certain types of cancer. Also promote strong bones and teeth.
Purple & Blue		Blackberries, blueberries,* black currants, eggplant,* plums, beets,* prunes and raisins.	Contain **anthocyanins** and **phenolics**. Lower the risk of cancer and heart disease. Also known to slow some effects of aging, such as memory loss.
White		Garlic, leeks and white onions.	Contain **allicin**, which may help reduce the spread of cancer and the risk of heart disease. Also may help fight infections.

These foods are particularly rich in antioxidants.
Some fruits and vegetables appear in more than one colour category because they are available in several varieties. Sources: pioneerthinking.com, consumerreports.org, 5to10aday.com.

ASIAN PANTRY

		Origins	Made from	How to use it
Soy Sauce or Shoyu		Japan, China	Dark, salty sauce made by fermenting boiled soybeans and roasted wheat or barley. Light soy sauce is thinner and saltier. Dark soy gets its colour from the addition of caramel. Chinese black soy is extremely dark and thick due to the addition of molasses.	Think of soy sauce as salt, and start with just a little.
Mirin		Japan	Used extensively in Japanese cooking, this low-alcohol, sweet, golden wine is made from glutinous rice. Sometimes referred to as rice wine or sake.	Adds sweetness and flavour. Use it in dressings, either on its own or blended with vinegars.
Red Curry Paste		Thailand	A mixture of dry chili pepper, shallot, garlic, galangal, lemongrass, cilantro root, peppercorn, coriander, salt, shrimp paste and kaffir lime zest.	Used as a base for sauces in Thai dishes.
Rice Vinegar		Japan	Made from fermented rice. Milder than most Western vinegars.	Use in salad dressings as you would any vinegar.
Hoisin Sauce		China	Sometimes referred to as Peking sauce, this thick, reddish-brown sauce is a sweet and spicy mixture of soybeans, garlic, chili peppers and various spices.	Used as a table condiment and flavouring agent for meat, poultry and shellfish dishes.
Oyster Sauce		China	A rich, dark-brown sauce consisting of oysters, brine and soy sauce cooked until thick and concentrated.	Imparts a richness to dishes without overpowering their natural flavour. Also used as a condiment.
Miso Paste		Japan	A fermented soybean paste with the consistency of peanut butter. Aged anywhere from six months to three years, it comes in many colours and flavours, and can vary from region to region.	Used in sauces, soups, marinades, dips, main dishes, salad dressings and as a condiment. Easily digested and extremely nutritious, with rich amounts of vitamin B and protein.
Dashi (instant)		Japan	A soup stock made with dried bonito tuna flakes, kelp and water. The instant form comes granulated or powdered, and is highly concentrated.	Add hot water, udon noodles, sautéed mushrooms and finely sliced green onions. Works beautifully with cooked meat, fish and seafood.
Noodles		China, Japan, Thailand, Korea, Indonesia, Vietnam, Philippines	Made from ingredients such as rice flour, potato flour, buckwheat flour, cornstarch and bean, yam or soybean starch.	Easy to prepare. Keep a variety on hand for soups, stews and stir-fries.
Coconut Milk		Thailand, Korea, Indonesia, Vietnam	Made by combining equal parts water and shredded, fresh coconut meat. It is simmered until foamy, then squeezed through cheesecloth to extract a thick liquid.	Adds richness to sauces, soups and desserts.
Fish Sauce		China	Juice extracted from fermented salted fish.	Use in very small portions just as you would salt. Heighten lazy flavours with just a dash.
Samba Oelek		Indonesia	A spicy prepared chili condiment.	Use in soups, rice and noodles. Adds heat without altering the original flavour.

into a large bowl of cold water to stop the cooking process. Cool completely and drain.

BONITO FLAKES
A small type of tuna, dried and shaved into large flakes, most commonly used for making dashi. It can also be sprinkled over vegetables or used to season tofu.

C

CHERMOULA [cher-MOO-la]
This paste, often used as a marinade or sauce, originated in North Africa and is a blend of coriander, parsley, lemon, olive oil and garlic. Works well with fish and meat.

CHIFFONADE
A method of chopping delicate, leafy herbs, such as basil, mint and sage, in order to minimize bruising and flavour loss. **How to:** Stack leaves of herb together and tightly roll into a cigar shape. With a sharp knife, slice crosswise to produce thin ribbons of the herb.

CLARIFY
A method of separating the fat, milk solids and water from butter. The golden liquid that results is widely used in cooking. **How to:** Bring unsalted butter to a boil, reduce heat to medium and skim foam from the top. Water and milk solids will separate to bottom of pan, leaving a clear liquid on top. Or you can purchase clarified butter (called ghee) from Indian grocery stores.

COMPOUND BUTTER
Butter creamed with other ingredients, like wine or herbs, to give it a sweet or savoury flavour.

CRÈME FRAÎCHE
A thickened cream with a slightly tangy, nutty flavour and velvety rich texture resembling that of sour cream. It's now available commercially, but you can make your own. **How to:** Add 2 tablespoons buttermilk to 1 cup of 35% cream. Store in a sealed glass jar and let stand in a warm area (like the top of your fridge) for 12 hours. Stir and store in fridge.

CRIMPING
Used to seal two layers of pastry together. It may be done with the tines of a fork, the back of a spoon or by pinching the dough with your fingertips.

D

DEGLAZE
Using a liquid to lift the sediment left behind in a hot pan after food has been cooked. The resulting flavourful concentration can be used in a sauce or for another part of the recipe. **How to:** Add a small amount of liquid (usually wine or stock) to the hot pan and stir to loosen the flavourful browned bits.

DREDGE
To lightly coat food with flour, cornmeal or bread crumbs prior to frying. This coating helps develop colour when cooking.

E

EGGS
All eggs sold in grocery stores in Canada are Grade A, which means the egg has a clean shell, is free of cracks, and has a well-centred yolk and a firm white. The colour of an egg's shell comes from the breed of hen that laid it and has no impact on its nutritional value. **Omega-3 eggs:** These eggs contain higher levels of omega-3 fatty acids that help lower triglyceride levels and may reduce the risk of heart disease. Hens are fed a diet with 10-20% ground flaxseed to increase omega-3 levels in their eggs. **Organic eggs:** Hens are fed certified organic grains. Look for a Certified Organic label. **Premium-quality eggs:** Taken from young hens during their peak laying period. These eggs have stronger shells, thicker whites and exceed Grade A quality. **Free-run eggs:** Hens can move freely about the barn and have access to nesting boxes and perches. **Free-range eggs:** Hens have access to outdoor runs. **Perfect poaching:** Fill a medium saucepan half-way with water, plus 1 tablespoon white vinegar and 1 tablespoon salt. Bring to a gentle simmer. Crack 2 eggs into a small bowl, making sure the yolks remain whole. Swirl the simmering water and gently slip eggs in, holding the bowl as close to the water as possible. Cook for 3 minutes for a delicate, runny yolk and tender white. Using a slotted spoon, remove eggs from water and tap the spoon on a tea towel to absorb excess water.

EGG WASH
Brushed on baked goods to give a golden finish. **How to:** Mix 1 egg yolk with 1 tablespoon water, cream or milk. Apply with a pastry brush before or during the cooking process.

EMULSIFY
To bring together an oil or fat with an acidic liquid (i.e. olive oil and vinegar) to get a thick, homogenous liquid, such as a vinaigrette or mayonnaise. **How to:** Vigorously whisk or shake until a thick sauce or dressing is achieved.

F

FATTY ACIDS
Omega-3s are a member of the so-called polyunsaturated fatty acid family (the other member is omega-6). They are necessary for growth and development, and produce compounds that influence blood pressure, cholesterol levels and kidney function, among other physiological functions.

FIBRE
Helps food move through the digestive system more rapidly and completely. Adding it to your diet can also help you keep your weight down and cholesterol levels under control. **1.** raspberries, blueberries. **2.** prunes, dates. **3.** cornmeal. **4.** navy beans, black beans. **5.** pumpkin seeds. **6.** avocado. **7.** dried figs. **8.** dried apricots. **9.** barley. **Insoluble fibre** comes from certain fruits and vegetables such as green beans, cauliflower, potato skins, popcorn, dried beans, seeds, brown rice and whole grain pastas, breads and cereals. This type of fibre provides bulk and assists in moving food through the digestive system. It is even thought to reduce the risk of colon cancer. **Soluble fibre** is found in prunes, apples, oranges, pears, peaches and grapes, as well as in dried beans, oatmeal, barley, rye, psyllium and vegetables such as

FIBRE SOURCES

carrots. This fibre mixes with liquids in the body and forms a gel-like substance, which soaks up cholesterol and exits the body as waste. Soluble fibre is known to prevent and control diabetes, as it slows the absorption of sugar.

FILET
A boneless piece of meat or fish.

FISH (portioning whole cooked fish, like char, salmon or trout)
Using a sharp knife, cut along the base of the head, down along the spine and across the top of the tail. Slowly pull the skin away, exposing tender cooked flesh. Portion generous pieces of fish and lift away from the bone until the entire spine is exposed. Remove bone by snapping it at base of head and gently lifting it off the remaining flesh. Portion the other side of the fish away from the skin with a spoon.

Removing skin.   Portioning fish.

Fish Serving Tray
A beautiful tray makes Salt-Baked Char look majestic but it can also be used for hors d'oeuvres, cutlery roll-ups, bread, cheese and much more. **How to: 1.** Cut a1 ½" to 2" thick piece of non-treated hardwood to approximately 10" x 28". **2.** Sand the top and sides of the wood to a smooth finish. **3.** Take two decorative kitchen door handles and place one at each end of the tray, approximately 4" in from the edge. **4.** Measure and mark for drilling. **5.** Drill holes for the screws and screw the handles into place. **6.** Rub the wood surface with block oil or canola oil to give it that deep rich finish. **7.** Attach small wooden or felt runners to the bottom of the board so it sits slightly elevated and gives the board a finished look. **8.** To maintain your board, gently wash with soapy water, rinse and dry well. Treat regularly with block or canola oil to prevent the wood from drying or splitting.

FLOUR
The type of flour you use will ultimately affect the finished product. Different types of flour contain different amounts of protein. The more protein, the denser the baking. Gluten is a protein in flour that develops elasticity when kneaded. It traps carbon dioxide, which allows bread to rise and gives it structure. **All-purpose:** Look for the unbleached kind whenever possible. The flavour is more natural and pure. Best for: Cakes, cookies, breads and pastries. **Bread flour:** Higher in gluten than all-purpose flour. Expect chewy results. You can substitute all-

purpose for bread, but not vice versa. Best for: Breads and pizza crusts. **Cake flour:** Velvety and fine in texture and very low in gluten. All-purpose flour is not a recommended substitute. Best for: Light and fluffy cakes and delicate-textured pastries. **Pastry flour:** Similar to cake flour, but not quite as fine in texture. Substituting cake for pastry and vice versa will work. Best for: Pastries, cookies and pies. **Self-rising:** This is essentially all-purpose flour with baking powder and salt added to it. Be sure to omit salt and baking powder from your recipe when using this variety. Best for: Baking. **Gluten-free:** Flour can be ground from more than just wheat. Trendy now because of their low-fat content, non-wheat flours have actually been milled for centuries. Varieties of gluten-free include buckwheat, chickpea, corn, potato, rice, soy, nut, legume, arrowroot, tapioca and even some vegetables.

FLOUR (baking tips)
Sifting: Removes lumps and aerates the flour so that when liquid is added, the dry ingredients get fully moistened. **Measuring:** Flour compacts easily. Too much flour will result in a tough baked good. Don't pack flour down into measuring cups. Spoon it in from the bag, tap cup to fill air holes and then level off with a knife. **Recipes:** If a recipe calls for a cup of sifted flour, sift the flour first and then measure one cup. If a recipe calls for one cup flour, sifted, sift the flour after it's been measured. **Storage:** Keep flour in a canister in a cool, dry and well-ventilated place for up to six months.

FOLD
To gently incorporate a light mixture into a denser mixture without losing volume. Use a spatula to incorporate ⅓ of light mixture at a time, combining by pulling mixture from sides into centre of bowl.

G
GINGER
Spicy aromatic root used to flavour both sweet and savoury dishes. **Benefits:** The use of ginger as a remedy for nausea and aid to digestion has been widely studied. It's believed ginger can also help fight off colds and, because it enhances circulation, ginger has been credited throughout history with increasing sex drive. The enzymes in ginger break down proteins and tenderize meats, making it an ideal ingredient for marinades. **Buying:** Look for pieces with a plump, smooth and somewhat shiny skin. Dried-out or shrivelled ginger will likely have a bitter, unpleasant aftertaste. Substituting powdered ginger for fresh does not give the same taste results. **Storing:** Store fresh ginger in a cool, dark place or for a short period of time in the refrigerator. **Preparing:** The fresher the ginger, the stronger the flavour. To peel fresh ginger, use a wishbone-shaped vegetable peeler, a small, sharp knife or the edge of a spoon. Ginger is very fibrous, so slice thinly when using. Smash slices to break up the fibres or use a traditional ginger grater for a very fine mince. **Powdered:** Like many spices, aroma and flavour are fragile, so buy in small quantities. Powdered ginger is available in many grades with some of the best coming from Jamaica. **Crystallized:** Because crystallized ginger won't sour milk, it's the perfect way to enhance the flavour of ice cream, custards and crème brulée. **Pickled:** Both the brilliant pink colour and tangy sweetness of pickled sushi ginger are artificially created. You can also find natural, pickled ginger. It is ivory in colour with no added preservatives.

GRAPESEED OIL

A clear, flavourless oil extracted by pressing the seeds of grapes. It can be used for dressings and vinaigrettes and, because it has a relatively high smoke point, it's also good for sautéing. It may be stored at room temperature or in the refrigerator.

GRATIN DISH

A shallow, ovenproof serving dish.

H

HOISIN

See Asian Pantry.

I

ICEWINE

A rich, sweet wine produced from grapes picked after they have frozen on the vine. It is high in both sugar and acid. **Quality control:** Canadian regulations state that the grapes cannot be artificially frozen.

K

KNEADING

Develops the gluten in the flour to form a network of strands that creates the elasticity necessary for bread to rise or stretch. **How to:** Use the heel of your hands, put your weight into it and push the dough away. Then fold it in half. Give it a slight turn and repeat.

KOMBU

A dark green, long, thick seaweed from the kelp family. Used frequently in Japanese cooking, it's an essential ingredient of dashi, a flavourful stock (see Asian Pantry).

L

LAMB (how to carve a bone-in leg)

Transfer cooked roast to a carving board, with the leg bone pointing left if you are right-handed. Hold the bone with a clean kitchen towel. Starting at the extreme right, slice downward at a slight angle and away from you, leaving slices attached to the bone. Run the knife along the top of the bone to detach slices. Transfer slices to a platter. Turn leg over and repeat on the other side.

LEMON OLIVE OIL

Olive oil that has been pressed or infused with fresh lemon. Available at most specialty food shops. Extra-virgin olive oil will work in a pinch.

LONG BEANS

Long, green beans found in Asian markets. You can also use regular string beans.

M

MINCE

A very fine chop, usually achieved by passing the blade of the knife through the food many times.

MIRIN

See Asian Pantry.

MORTAR & PESTLE

The mortar is shaped like a bowl and the pestle is a blunt piece of wood or stone used to pulverize seeds, herbs and nuts. The grinding action releases the oils and flavourful essences.

MUSHROOMS (cleaning)

Never soak mushrooms in water – they are very absorbant and will become soggy. Instead, simply use a mushroom brush or wipe with a damp paper towel. If mushrooms are very dirty, you can rinse them under cold running water and blot with a towel.
1. Chanterelle: Buttery soft flesh, fruity in aroma and slightly peppery in taste. Fresh chanterelles should be plump and somewhat firm to the touch. Available fresh during fall and winter.
2. Shiitake: Slightly chewy texture and smoky flavour. Look for firm caps without dark or wet spots, with edges that curl under. Fresh are available year round. The stems are a little woody but packed with flavour. Save them for flavouring stocks and sauces.
3. Button: Mild flavour and tender texture. The most popular

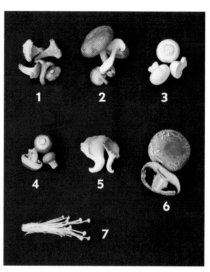

by far, this variety is a kitchen staple. They're great raw or cooked, and you can buy them fresh year round. Hand select as opposed to buying pre-packaged.
4. Cremini: More intense earthy flavour than the common button mushroom. Look for a firm, dry mushroom. Fresh year round.
5. Oyster: These mushrooms have a velvety smooth texture and delicate flavour, and are best cooked. When purchasing, look for clusters. Fresh year round.
6. Portobello: A member of the cremini family – large with a hearty flavour and meaty texture. Great for grilling and roasting. Look for dry, unbroken gills.
7. Enoki: Mild and delicate in flavour. Can be eaten raw and often found in Asian cooking. Texture like al dente pasta.

N

NORI

Sheets of toasted seaweed, rich in calcium, iron, proteins, vitamins and minerals, with a subtle flavour.

O

OFF-SET SPATULA

Unlike a rubber spatula, this handy tool has a stiff metal blade that bends up where it meets a wooden handle (hence the term "off-set"). It's great for getting underneath tricky foods like pancakes or delicate fish, sliding cookies off a baking sheet or icing cakes.

OMEGA-3 FATTY ACIDS

Beneficial for those with high cholesterol and cardiovascular disease, Omega-3s are not manufactured by the body – the only way to get them is through your diet. The recommended daily requirement of omega-3s is at least 0.65 g. The examples on the following page are easy to find and easy to cook:

OMEGA-3 SOURCES

1. **1 cup purslane:** 1 g omega-3 (7 calories)
2. **¼ cup flaxseed:** 7 g omega-3 (236 calories)
3. **4 oz. salmon (baked or broiled):** 2 g omega-3 (207 calories)
4. **¼ cup walnuts :** 2 g omega-3 (186 calories)
   and **¼ cup pecans:** 0.2 g omega-3 (201 calories)
5. **2 tbsp. canola oil:** 2.5 g omega-3 (240 calories)
6. **1 egg (omega-3-fortified):** 0.5 g omega-3 (73 calories)
7. **3 oz. bison:** 1.3 g omega-3 (145 calories)
8. **4 oz. sea scallops:** 1 g omega-3 (100 calories)
9. **1 cup soybeans (cooked):** 1 g omega-3 (300 calories)

P

PANKO
Sweet, white Japanese breadcrumbs.

PARBOIL/PARCOOK
To partially cook a food item to either help in preparation or to reduce a cooking time later, such as roasted vegetables, pasta or French fries.

POTATOES (how to store)
Store in a cool, dark place with good air circulation. Do not refrigerate, as the starches will turn to sugar – and keep them away from your onions. Onions release a chemical that causes potatoes to sprout.

Type of Potato	Bake	Roast	Boil	Fries	Mash
Idaho	✓	✓	✓		✓
Fingerling	✓	✓	✓		
Red-skinned		✓	✓		
New		✓	✓		
Yukon Gold	✓	✓	✓	✓	✓
Sweet Potato	✓	✓	✓	✓	✓
Russet	✓		✓	✓	✓

Type of Bird	Size Matters	How Much to Get	Healthy Rewards	What Came First? A Bit About the Egg
Quail	5-10 oz.	2-3 birds per person	Rich in protein and relatively low in fat.	Delicate and easily found in Chinese grocers. Serve hard-boiled on your next salad.
Cornish Hen	1-2 lbs.	½-1 bird per person	Good source of vitamin B$_6$, phosphorus, zinc and potassium	Too young for eggs.
Chicken	2-4 lbs.	½ lb. per person, uncooked	Raw chicken contains less fat than red meat, but the same amount of cholesterol. Rich in protein, niacin and vitamin B$_6$.	Farm-fresh eggs make a real difference to your omelettes or baked goods.
Duck	4-7 lbs.	1-1½ lbs. per person, uncooked	Rich in iron and B complex vitamins.	Found in Chinese supermarkets, duck eggs are larger than chicken eggs.
Goose	6-11 lbs.	1-1½ lbs. per person, uncooked	Similar to duck but more fatty.	Very similar in taste to chicken and duck eggs, but not as readily available.
Capon	8-10 lbs.	½ lb. per person, uncooked	Tastes like chicken.	A male bird, so no eggs found here.
Turkey	7-20 lbs.	1-1½ lbs. per person, uncooked	High in protein, niacin, vitamin B$_6$, zinc and potassium.	Turkeys produce half the number of eggs chickens do. Most turkey eggs are only used to produce more turkeys.

POULTRY (see chart on previous page)
Handling: Let frozen birds thaw completely in the fridge. Remove fresh or thawed birds from store packaging, cover loosely and refrigerate until ready to use. Store in the coldest part of the fridge. Wash hands thoroughly after handling. Wash and rinse surfaces raw bird comes in contact with. **Equipment:** Meat thermometer, roasting pan with a lid and rack, butcher's twine, carving knife and fork, oven mitts. **More gadgets:** Mesh bags for stuffing, disposable pop-up temperature gauge, measuring cup that separates fat from gravy, poultry shears, electric carving knife. **When it's done:** Insert thermometer into thigh of bird without hitting the bone. At 165 F, juices will run clear and meat should be moist and tender. Allow bird to rest before carving.

PURSLANE
A succulent, sprawling plant with a mild, sweet-sour flavour and a chewy texture. Contains more omega-3s than any other leafy green.

Q
QUINOA
A grain that is lower in carbs and higher in protein than most. A great rice alternative, fantastic in salads and gluten free.

R
RAMEKIN
A small porcelain ovenproof baking dish, usually 3 to 4 inches in diameter. They're used mainly for baked custard and egg dishes.

RAMPS
Also known as wild leeks, these tender leafy members of the onion family have a bold garlic-onion flavour and are available only in early spring.

RICE-PAPER WRAPPERS
The edible, translucent paper is made from rice flour. The paper comes in various sizes, can be found in fine-food stores and Asian markets, and is most often used to wrap foods to be eaten raw or deep-fried.

S
SAMBAL OELEK
See Asian Pantry.

SALT
Salt comes from salt mines, large deposits left by dried salt lakes or from seawater. **Table salt** is refined with additives that make it free flowing. **Sea salt** results from evaporated seawater, available fine-grained or as large crystals. **Kosher salt** is mined, free of additives and is coarse-grained. It is half as salty as sea salt and is used in some Jewish preparations of meats. Because of its texture and subtle flavour, we find kosher salt allows the true flavours of the ingredients to really stand out.
Other salts we adore to pour:
• **Red** (or Hawaiian) has a reddish-orange colour from the lava of Kauai and Molokai. It has a mellow, earthy flavour.

• **Fleur de Sel** is raked from the shore near the village of Guerande in Brittany. It dries in the sun and forms crystal "flowers." Slightly moist and pinkish-grey in colour, it's considered an extravagance, sprinkled on a dish at the last minute so that its flavour and texture can be savoured.
• **Maldon**, from the English coast, resembles large flakes, is briney in taste and great over fresh vegetables.
• **Sel Marin**, a grey sea salt from Brittany, is dirty grey in colour, moist to the touch and has a high content of magnesium and other minerals.

SAUTERNES [so-TERN]
A sweet wine from the Sauternes region of France, made from Sauvignon Blanc or Sémillon grapes. Sauternes is often thought of as a dessert wine but, because of its high acidity, it is also an excellent match for rich foods like pâté, caviar and foie gras.

SEGMENT
A segment of citrus fruit should be free of peel and membrane. **How to:** Cut off the top and bottom of fruit exposing its flesh. Using a serrated paring knife, slice the peel away from sides, following the curve of the fruit. All peel and membrane should be removed. To release individual segments, slide knife down both sides of membrane.

SNAP PEAS/SNOWPEAS (de-stringing)
The pea pod has a fibrous seam that should be removed before eating. After washing, snap off the stem ends, using them to pull off the string.

STEAK (grilling)
Since each barbecue has its own unique level of heat, cooking times are generally variable. As you continue to perfect your craft and learn when to pull steak off the grill, don't be afraid to peek and cheat – make a small incision into whatever you're cooking and see where it's at. Even chefs sometimes use the knife test. This allows you to become comfortable with cooking times, colours and the feel for what you are cooking. Allowing meats to rest is key to delivering a perfectly grilled steak. Serve 5-10 minutes after barbecuing. See next page for choice cuts.

GRILLING CHART

THICKNESS	VERY RARE	RARE	MEDIUM RARE	WELL DONE
1 inch	8 minutes	9 minutes	11 minutes	15-18 minutes
1 ½ inches	8-10 minutes	10-12 minutes	13-15 minutes	15-20 minutes
2 inches	14-18 minutes	18-25 minutes	25 minutes	30-45 minutes
2 ½ inches	20-25 minutes	25-35 minutes	35-40 minutes	45-60 minutes
3 inches + – *use a meat thermometer*	120-130 F	125-135 F	145-160 F	170 F+

STEAK (choice cuts)

Flank: This inexpensive boneless cut is best marinated. Think 4-8 ounces per person. To serve, thinly slice across the grain.

Striploin, a.k.a. New York: Look for well-marbled steaks. This cut has great flavour and doesn't need to be marinated.

T-bone, a.k.a. Porterhouse: This bone-in, expensive cut has both a section from the tenderloin and striploin attached. You'll need at least 1 pound per person due to the weight of the bone.

Tenderloin, a.k.a. Filet Mignon: The most tender and expensive, but may be not the most flavourful – one of the reasons it is often served wrapped in bacon.

Rib Eye: This cut is tender and flavourful. Choose steaks with minimal outside fat.

SUNDRIED TOMATO
Tomatoes that have been dried in the sun resulting in a chewy, intensely flavourful, dark red tomato. Sundried tomatoes add a rich flavour to sauces, soups, sandwiches, salads and pasta dishes. Available packed in oil or dry (rehydrate before using by cooking in oil or water).

SUSHI
The term means "seasoned rice" and refers to the sushi bar or shop where patrons go to watch master sushi chefs at work.

SUSHI RICE
A short-grained, starchy rice used specifically for making sushi.

SWEAT
To bring out the natural juices of an ingredient by cooking over medium-low heat without browning, using very little oil or butter.

T

TENDERLOIN
The most coveted cut of beef, pork and lamb. This term also refers to the tender strip found in poultry breasts, which sits directly on the breastbone and pulls away easily from the rest of the breast.

TOMATOES
1. Heirloom: These varieties are often over 50 years in age, the seeds harvested and handed down through generations to preserve the characteristics of the original plants. They are well worth seeking out while in season. Best for: Slicing and eating on their own or in a simple salad to fully appreciate their unique taste.
2. Cherry tomatoes: The smallest of the bunch. This variety ranges in shape from grape to pear to cherry. Colours range from yellow to orange to red. Best for: Salads and pastas – and just popping in your mouth for a burst of flavour.
3. Vine-ripened: Available in the grocery store all year long and commonly grown in hot-houses, this variety comes in yellow, orange and red. Best for: Use during the winter when field tomatoes are not in season.
4. Roma/Plum: Egg-shaped, meaty and low in moisture, Romas are generally available year round. Best for: Sauces, canning and tomato paste. Romas also star in caprese salads in the height of their season.

5. Beefsteak/Field: One of the largest varieties in size and bright red in colour, hearty beefsteaks are readily available in late summer and fall. Best for: Slicing and great for sandwiches.

V

VERMICELLI
Italian for "little worms," this noodle is much thinner than spaghetti. Italian vermicelli is made with semolina and the Asian version, also known as rice noodle, is made with rice flour. **How to cook Asian vermicelli:** Place noodles in a bowl and cover with boiling water. Set aside and allow to soak for 10 minutes or so. Drain.

VITAMIN C
Known as ascorbic acid, Vitamin C is a water-soluble antioxidant vitamin essential to the body's health. It acts as a natural antihistamine, lessening the severity of colds; stimulates the immune system; helps keep gums healthy; can help prevent stroke, heart attack and certain cancers; and aids in collagen production, which is a necessary fibre in the body's connective tissue and cartilage – helping skin stay healthy and younger looking. **Key sources:** Avocados, broccoli, oranges, Brussels sprouts, cauliflower, grapefruit, persimmons, sweet potatoes, tomatoes and kiwi.

W

WASABI
A very hot Japanese horseradish. Purchase as a powder or paste. Add a small amount to soy dipping sauce to spice things up.

Z

ZEST
The brightly coloured outer skin of citrus fruits containing pure, concentrated oils. When zesting lemons, oranges or limes, use a grater, rasp or zester to remove only the outer peel, not the white pith, which is very bitter.

TOMATO VARIETIES

acknowledgements

Wish Team
This book was made possible through the huge efforts of the entire team throughout our inaugural year. Special thanks to everyone who continues to dot our i's, cross our t's – and test our cookies: Ruth Alves, Giorgina Bigioni, Margot Bolin, Bonnie Brownlee, Luigi Carrubba, Catherine Franklin, Patricia Gajo, Genevieve Gately, Alan Gomez, Jane Hardin, Tory Healy, Andrea Janus, Sandy Kim, Alison Lawler-Dean, Ashleigh McKenna, Carlo Mendoza, Andrea Mills, Aimee Nishitoba, Lorenzo Sechi for Pi Media, Doug Wallace.

Behind the Scenes
Our food stylists, prop stylists, recipe testers, nutritionists, contributing photographers, writers and assistants continually inspire us and help bring our ideas to life: Kimberlee Ashby, Kester Birch, Michaela Cornell, Jenn Cranston, Carol Dudar, Ruth Gangbar, Hannah Guy, Sue Henderson, Marc Joliat, Emilios Kattides, Hamin Lee, Lara McGraw, Felice Morsillo, Ian Muggridge, Daphna Rabinovitch, Lucie Richard, Adele Rogers, Amy Snider, Kimberley Stewart, Helen Stubbs, Tom Thai, Nora Underwood, LeeAnne Wright.

A sincere thank you to friends, family and colleagues for sharing the secrets of their recipe box: Phyllis Bigioni, Pasta e Fagioli, 66. Pina Carrubba, Spinach Crepe Manicotti, 92. Mary Clark, Scottish Tablet, 115. Louise Dimma, Rainy-day Eggs, 18. Mary Dooher, Italian Wedding Soup, 67. Elizabeth Francisco, Dutch Chocolate Cake, 106. Claudette Franklin, Mushroom Oregano Rice, 58. Ok Nam Kim, Spicy Korean Chicken Pot, 94. LeeAnne Wright, Chipotle Garlic Rub, 42; Moroccan Quinoa Salad, 67; Masala Orange Zest Rub, 139; Smoky Citrus Rub, 141.

We are very grateful for the hard work and support of our partners at CanWest: Leah Campbell, Kerry MacGregor, Lynn McAuley, Carole-Ann Hayes and Tracy Nixon. We also thank Felicia Quon and the team at HarperCollins.

Special Favours, Special Thanks
It's nice to know you can rely on the kindness of friends (and friends of friends): David Bagosy, Julia Francisco, Sandor Gregorin, Dwight Ireland, Laurie Jennings, Leanne Johnston, Laura Keogh, Shari Monahar, Alison Vieira and everyone at The Cookworks and Mildred Pierce Restaurant.

Get the Look
Presentation isn't everything, but it sure helps make a meal or an event feel more special. If you're interested in any of the gorgeous dishware, utensils and other kitchenware you've seen on these pages, visit **wish.ca/cookbook** to find out where to buy them.

Subscribe to Wish
Have every issue of **wish** magazine delivered right to your doorstep. Visit us at **wish.ca** and take advantage of our best subscription offers. A year of **wish** is also a perfect gift.

Photography

Nothing makes your mouth water like a beautiful picture of food – you can almost taste it.
Thanks to the talented photographers who make us look so delicious:

Michael Alberstat
4, 10, 18, 19, 22, 32, 35,
36, 44, 45, 54, 57, 58, 59,
66, 85, 86, 93, 94, 95, 103,
107, 121, 137, back cover

Douglas Bradshaw
cover, 58

Chris Chapman
46, 47, 49, 50, 51

Colin Faulkner
6, 14, 38, 39, 55, 68, 69, 70,
71, 72, 73, 83, 86, 141

Rob Fiocca
11, 60, 61, 94, 96, 97, 98, 99,
100, 101, 104, 115, 119, 123,
127, 133

Andrew Grinton
108, 112

Rob Kinghorn
13, 22, 31, 33, 37, 43, 53, 62,
66, 91, 95, 105, 114, 138

Mark Olson
82

Edward Pond
7, 16, 88, 89, 116, 117

James Tse
9, 14, 15, 17, 21, 23, 40, 41,
44, 63, 65, 67, 81, 90, 108,
109, 113, 121, 125, 128, 129,
135, 139, 141, 142

George Whiteside
24, 25, 26, 29, 74, 75, 77,
78, 79, 87

index

Oven Temperatures

Imperial	Metric
120 F	50 C
130 F	55 C
150 F	65 C
200 F	100 C
225 F	110 C
250 F	120 C
275 F	140 C
300 F	150 C
325 F	160 C
350 F	180 C
375 F	190 C
400 F	200 C
425 F	220 C
450 F	230 C
475 F	240 C
500 F	260 C

Mass (Weight)

Imperial	Metric
1 oz.	30 g
2 oz.	60 g
3 oz.	90 g
4 oz. (¼ lb.)	125 g
5 oz.	150 g
⅓ lb.	170 g
6 oz.	175 g
8 oz. (½ lb.)	250 g
10 oz.	300 g
⅔ lb.	350 g
12 oz. (¾ lb.)	375 g
1 lb. (16 oz.)	500 g
1 ¼ lbs.	625 g
1 ½ lbs.	750 g
1 ¾ lbs.	875 g
2 lbs.	1 kg
3 lbs.	1.5 kg
4 lbs.	2 kg
5 lbs.	2.2 kg
6 lbs.	2.7 kg
7 lbs.	3.15 kg
8 lbs.	3.5 kg
9 lbs.	4 kg
10 lbs.	4.5 kg

Volume Measurements

Imperial	Metric
¼ tsp.	1 ml
½ tsp.	2 ml
¾ tsp.	4 ml
1 tsp.	5 ml
2 tsp.	10 ml
1 tbsp.	15 ml
2 tbsp.	25 ml
3 tbsp.	45 ml
¼ cup	50 ml
⅓ cup	75 ml
½ cup	125 ml
⅔ cup	150 ml
¾ cup	175 ml
1 cup	250 ml
2 cups	500 ml
3 cups	750 ml
4 cups	1 L
5 cups	1.25 L
6 cups	1.5 L
7 cups	1.75 L
8 cups	2 L

Quick Conversions

3 tsp. = 1 tbsp.

4 tbsp. = ¼ cup

4 cups = 1 L

8 oz. = ½ lb.

8 fluid oz. = 1 cup

500 g = 1 lb.

1 kg = 2.2 lbs.

Common Package Sizes

Imperial	Metric
4 oz.	114 ml
5 ½ oz.	156 ml
7 ½ oz.	213 ml
10 oz.	285 ml
14 oz.	398 ml
19 oz.	540 ml
28 oz.	796 ml

Cooking & Bakeware

Cake Pans (Metal)
8" (2 L) square
9" (2.5 L) square
11" x 7" (2 L)
13" x 9" (3.5 L)
8" (1.2 L) round
9" (1.5 L) round

Baking Dishes (Glass)
8" (2 L) square
11" x 7" (2 L)
11" x 9" (2.5 L)
12" x 8" (3 L)
13" x 9" (3 L)
10" (3 L) oval

Soufflé Dishes
7" x 3" (1.5 L)
8" x 3 ¾ " (2.5 L)

Loaf Pans
5" x 3" (625 ml)
8" x 4" (1.5 L)
9" x 5" (2 L)
10" x 6" (3 L)

Springform Pans
6" (1.25 L)
7" (1.5 L)
8" (2 L)
8 ½" (2.25 L)
9" (2.5 L)
10" (3 L)
11" (3.5 L)

**Ramekins/
Custard Cups**
3" (125 ml)
6 oz. (175 ml)

Tube Pans
9" (3 L)
10" (4 L)
10" Bundt Pan (3 L)

Rimmed Baking Sheets
(formerly known
as Jelly Roll Pans)
15" x 10" (40 x 25 cm)
17" x 11" (45 x 29 cm)

Pie Plates
9" (23 cm)
10" (25 cm)

French Tart Pans (With
Removable Bottoms)
9" (23 cm)
10" (25 cm)
11" (28 cm)
11" x 8" (28 x 20 cm)
14" x 4" (35 x 10 cm)

EDITOR Jane Francisco
ART DIRECTOR Sandy Kim
EXECUTIVE EDITOR Doug Wallace
FOOD EDITORS Donna Dooher, Andrea Stewart
HOME DESIGN EDITOR Suzanne Dimma
ASSOCIATE ART DIRECTOR Ruth Alves
ASSISTANT FOOD EDITOR Tory Healy
ASSISTANT EDITOR, COPY Andrea Janus

COVER
Photography by Douglas Bradshaw
Food Styling by Ruth Gangbar
Stacked BLT & Avocado Salad (page 58)

BACK COVER
Photography by Michael Alberstat